"Steve is a very experienced businessman who has applied the principles you will learn in *Roadmap to Success*. Steve has dedicated his life to teaching people in the business community God's way of operating a business. If you're considering building a business, I recommend you read this book before making that decision. I deeply admire Steve Marr, and you will appreciate this practical message."

– Howard Dayton,
Co-founder of Crown Financial Ministries

"*Roadmap to Success* is long overdue and a much needed primer for Christians considering starting a new business. Please read it carefully and prayerfully before you jump!"

– Dennis Peacocke,
Founder and President of Strategic Christian Services

"Stop! Do not start your business until you read Steve Marr's *Roadmap to Success*. Your dream could become a nightmare if you do not seek biblical counsel. The assessments alone are worth purchasing this book. These practical suggestions will save you thousands of dollars and help you in achieving profitability."

– Kent Humphreys,
President of FCCI / Christ@Work

"In my experience of working with numerous business authors and experts, Steve Marr is the most gifted man I've ever met in terms of his ability to bring God's wisdom to practical application at every level in business. *Roadmap to Success* not only offers God-given biblical principles for launching a new venture, but it's also a must read for those who are already running a business and want to make sure that their business is based on a biblical foundation."

– Joe Johnson,
Founder and President of Business Reform *magazine*

D0964711

"Steve Marr's book is a must read for anyone considering the high calling of starting and operating a business. This book provides practical insights, knowledge, and biblical principles that will assist any entrepreneur with the needed guidance for being eternally successful."

–Scott McFarlane
Executive Director of Evangelical Commerce Institute

"*Roadmap to Success* is a must-have for anyone starting or reevaluating their business. The author touches on subjects that we do not even realize affect our businesses. From marriage and family considerations to finding office space to rent, the author takes you through a process that will help you achieve the security and foundation you will need to run your business God's way and maintain a healthy balance between family and career."

–Kathleen Jackson
Publisher of The Godly Business Woman *Magazine*

"Getting started on a project in the right way can make all the difference in the world to how you will finish. Success or failure is built in early. Like in life, your first steps in starting a business matter. In *Roadmap to Success*, Steve Marr helps you discover how to lead with the right steps toward success in your business. It's worth your time to read this one!"

–Dr. Randy Carlson
President of Family Life Radio Network

"With Scripture as the cornerstone, Steve Marr offers simple, practical steps to lay the foundation for a successful and faith-filled business. *Roadmap to Success* is for anyone who dares to dream of starting their own business, but has the humility and courage to recognize it can't be done without God's guidance. If you are starting a business or know someone who is, this is the book to read."

–Paul J. Meyer, Founder of Success Motivation Institute, Inc.,
and 40+ other companies and New York Times *best-selling author*

Roadmap to SUCCESS

Roadmap to SUCCESS

BUILDING YOUR BUSINESS GOD'S WAY

by Steve Marr

Bridge-Logos
Gainesville, Florida 32614

Bridge-Logos
Gainesville, FL 32614 USA

Roadmap to Success
by Steve Marr

Printed in the United States of America.

Library of Congress Catalog Card Number: 2005933299
International Standard Book Number 0-88270-035-9

Scriptures noted KJV are taken from the KING JAMES VERSION of the Bible.

Scriptures noted NKJV are taken from the NEW KING JAMES VERSION. Copyright © 1979, 1980, 1982, Thomas Nelson, Inc., Publishers. Used by permission. All rights reserved.

Scriptures noted NASB are taken from the New American Standard Bible®. Copyright © 1960,1962,1963,1968,1972,1975,1977,1995 by The Lockman Foundation. Used by permission. All rights reserved.

Scriptures noted NIV are taken from the Holy Bible, New International Version®. NIV®. Copyright © 1973, 1978, 1984 by International Bible Society. Used by permission of Zondervan Publishing House. All rights reserved.

Scriptures noted NRSV are taken from the New Revised Standard Version. Copyright © 1989 by the Division of Christian Education of the National Council of the Churches of Christ in the United States of America. Used by permission. All rights reserved.

Scripture quotations marked (NLT) are taken from the Holy Bible, New Living Translation, copyright © 1996. Used by permission of Tyndale House Publishers, Inc., Wheaton, Illinois 60189. All rights reserved.

G1.316.N.m509.35250

Acknowledgements

I want to express thanks to the Good Lord, Jesus Christ, without whose lordship and leadership in my life this book would not have been possible. Also, for God's Word that contains every truth we need to live a successful and blessed life, including in our business lives.

My wife, Mary has been a consistent source of encouragement to me to follow through with the project vision and she has been a great helpmate.

Also, I would like to express appreciation to Michael Marshall for the technical and graphic support for the Business Proverbs Ministry, and Merlynn Hanson for her administrative support.

I am grateful for the assistance of Brian Mast for his help in editing and layout design of the book and for his feedback. I appreciate the dozens of people who read all or part of the manuscript and provided candid feedback helping to improve the finished product.

I thank the clients and business leaders who have furnished the true stories and much of the material in this book. The names, places, and companies have all been changed to protect their confidentiality.

Table of Contents

Foreword

Millions of people dream of opening their own business and becoming successful. The hard reality is that each year, of the 700,000 large and small businesses started each year, 50% will fail. What remains is usually a large swath of personal devastation, fractured relationships, and financial carnage.

Whether you are just starting out or wanting to grow your business, this book is focused on a biblically based roadmap for success. As you read, you'll notice that I've pointed out some roadblocks and bad accidents. They're warnings to slow down and re-think your plans. In these cases, I'll give you alternate routes and show you how to avoid becoming another tragic statistic. More than that, I'll show you how to achieve success.

The prophet Joshua said, *"This book of the law shall not depart from your mouth, but you shall meditate on it day and night, so that you may be careful to do according to all that is written in it; for then you will make your way prosperous, and then you will have success"* (Joshua 1:8, NASB).

The promise from the Lord is that if we read His Word and choose to be obedient, then we are promised success, which is a blessing from the Lord. I do not believe we are promised to become after millionaires, but to have a happy, blessed life when we are obedient.

Scripture gives us inspired truth we need to apply to every aspect of life, including business. Many leading figures in the Bible built great enterprises with God's help. Abraham built great flocks (a rancher) and Joseph administrated all of Egypt preparing for a great famine (a warehouse manager). Noah built a great ark (a shipping company) while King Solomon built a great empire using wisdom granted by God.

Being in business has its challenges, as every business owner understands. Owners are required to wear many hats, and wear them well. The statistics show that most business fail and those that do survive usually generate meager returns.

The focus of this book is to assist you in preparing your own road map to success following principles outlined in the Bible. It's your dream and agenda, and this map will help you get there. Most of us pull out a map when starting on a driving vacation to make sure we reach our destination as quickly as possible. Similarly, starting or growing your business with a map will save you time, energy, and disappointment. I have used Scriptures from several translations, including the KJV, NKJV, NIV, NASB, NLT and NRSV. In study, I find that using several translations assists in increasing understanding from His Word.

My prayer is that you will use this book as road map to help discover God's perfect will for your life and business endeavor. His children should experience nothing less.

CHAPTER 1

Choosing Your Cornerstone

Martha could not sleep all night. The excitement over the grand opening of her business tomorrow was just too much. Years of dreaming, months of planning and the weeks spent getting everything ready would soon start paying off. Customers would flock to buy the great decorative items in her store.

The next morning at nine o'clock, Martha turned the front door sign from closed to open and anticipated the first ringing of the cash register. Enthusiasm began to wane by eleven o'clock as no one had entered the store. That afternoon a few friends had stopped by and several customers had purchased $87.76 of merchandise.

The shop's location, while inexpensive, was in an older part of town and failed to attract the needed traffic. Many who stopped by were not interested in her trendy artwork and decorative items.

Over the first six months sales averaged less than 20% of what was needed to break even, quickly eating into her cash reserves. Martha tried a few ads but with poor results.

Since all her funds were exhausted on the one-year anniversary of her store, Martha obtained a second mortgage on her home and became extended with credit cards as she struggled to keep her dream afloat.

Before the second anniversary she closed the business after racking up losses of $170,000. She owed more than her house was worth plus $70,000 on her credit cards. To make matters worse, the landlord reminded her that she had personally guaranteed the five-year lease and he expected payment each month and would sue to collect if necessary. Defeated, emotionally empty, and bankrupt— Martha was now out of business. What went wrong?

God Wants You To Succeed

Every enterprise starts with a dream. Following the right process will make the difference between seeing your dreams fulfilled or waking up in a nightmare like Martha.

God does not want any of His children to fail. God reassuringly states, "For surely I know the plans I have for you, says the LORD, plans for your welfare and not for harm, to give you a future with hope" (Jeremiah 29:11, NRSV). The Lord wants only the best for all His children.

> **The fact that God wants you to succeed is a truth as much as it is a mindset.**

In order to experience God's best, we must first discover God's perfect will for our lives. His process is an orderly process, and if we are willing to follow that process faithfully, then He will be able to bless our endeavors.

Choosing Obedience

When you believe God is leading you into a business begin by deciding to bring every action into agreement with God's Scriptures. Many people in business offer only half-hearted obedience; they follow the Lord when the circumstances are convenient.

Consider Amaziah, king of Judah. Scriptures say, *"He did what was right in the eyes of the LORD, but not wholeheartedly"* (2 Chronicles 25:2, NIV). While Amaziah won victories against his enemies, he ultimately lost everything, including his freedom, because of his disobedience.

Joshua 1:7 states, *"Be strong and very courageous. Be careful to obey all the law my servant Moses gave you; do not turn from it to the right or to the left, that you may be successful wherever you go"* (NIV).

Obedience to God's will brings blessings, while disobedience brings failure. Though a business failure, such as what Martha experienced, may be the result of a combination of errors (i.e. bad location, lack of reserves, etc.), obedience to God is the first place to start when planning for business success.

Committing All To Prayer

Jesus said, *"If you believe, you will receive whatever you ask for in prayer"* (Matthew 21:22, NIV). Therefore, if we believe we are called to become an owner or steward of a business, we first need to seek God's wisdom, guidance, and perfect process through prayer.

God will answer every prayer. He answers with "yes," "no," or "wait." By committing every step of your business process to prayer, you will be able to discern God's answer. Many people tell God what they want to do and then ask Him to bless their plans. But Jesus said, *"You shall not put the Lord your God to the test"* (Matthew 4:7, NASB).

Dr. James Dobson of *Focus On the Family* teaches that "our emotions will fool us every time," So, we must guard against the trap of excessive emotionalism as a guide for our decisions. Instead, we need to specifically ask the Lord in prayer whether or not we should embark on a particular business venture — and then wait for the answer.

Prayer is the only effective tool that will help us discern God's perfect will.

• Examining the evidence is not enough

The leaders of Israel decided to make a peace treaty with a group after believing the group had come from a long distance. The leaders based their belief on the "evidence" that the group had traveled far by examining their stale bread, cracked wineskins and worn clothing.

However, they made a bad decision. *"The men of Israel sampled their provisions but did not inquire of the LORD"* (Joshua 9:14, NIV). Likewise, when we examine only the evidence, and do not consult the Lord, we can miss God's will.

In one instance I invested money in a fish farm. I have always liked fishing and I have enjoyed having an aquarium. I studied the business plan, met the management, and reviewed the property. I examined the evidence. I took every step but the most important one. I failed to ask the Lord for guidance. I entered into the transaction entirely in my own strength.

Within the first year of my investment, I began to see that the management was weak, regularly shaded the truth, and could not execute an effective business plan. As a result, the entire project was sinking into oblivion, taking my investment with it.

> **LOCATION & TIMING!**
> **They either spell**
> **success or disaster.**

I prayed to the Lord and asked Him to get me out of this mess, to reverse my situation. The Lord answered by asking, "Did you seek me before you got into this mess?" I confessed I had not. The Lord impressed on me that if I got into situations in my own strength, then I would need to get out in my own strength. I have experienced instances where the

Lord steps in and rescues me or rescues other people, but there are times (because God knows we need a hard lesson) that we live with the consequences of our mistakes.

The Lord taught me a lesson I intend to never forget. Ask the Lord first!

• God's timing is critical

Even when we receive a yes from God, we must continue in prayer, being careful not to run ahead, insisting on our own timing rather than on God's timing. In Habakkuk 2:3 the great prophet warns, *"For the vision is yet for the appointed time; It hastens toward the goal, and it will not fail. Though it tarries, wait for it; For it will certainly come, it will not delay"* (NASB). The execution of our vision must line up with God's timing.

Connor wanted to open a vegetable market in his town. He took the steps to investigate leasing store space and obtaining the business licenses. As he continued in prayer for God's perfect will, obstacle after obstacle began to appear. For example, the prospective landlord failed to honor promises for improvements before Connor was to sign the lease. The city's largest employer announced his plant was closing, putting 25% of the population out of work. Fortunately, because Conner had stayed in prayer for guidance, he immediately halted the store project. By responding correctly to the delay, Connor experienced God's protection.

Five years later, after new businesses moved into town and employment rose to previous levels, the town recovered from the economic shock. Connor was now able to take the steps to open the vegetable market. Because it was God's perfect timing, the effort went smoothly and was successful. Had Connor started five years earlier, the result would most likely have been bankruptcy.

Passion Must Be Present

You must have a passion for whatever business you choose in order to be successful. Passion fuels faithfulness when times get tough.

Dave loved bread. He cherished kneading bread, holding it, watching it rise, and baking it while enjoying the aroma. Dave enjoyed every aspect of bread. He thrived on seeing people line up for samples and delighted in his customers enjoying the products. In short, Dave had a passion for bread and everything about bread. That passion carried Dave through the challenges of owning his own business and empowered him to rise at 3:00 a.m. to start his day. Passion was a key factor in Dave owning a successful bakery.

Sue and Bill wanted to open a specialty ice cream and yogurt business. Their goal was to build a business that would produce income but would require little hands-on participation. They came to me for advice on how best to open the business. My first questions were, "Do you like ice cream? Do you like to scoop it out? Do you like to make sundaes and milk shakes? Do you enjoy watching customers eat ice cream?"

Bill responded that those were not important issues to them. Both he and Sue intended to hire a staff to run the place and did not plan on scooping ice cream themselves. They were surprised at my advice. I strongly recommended they not start an ice cream business. I explained, that realistically, they would need to spend time in the store, training staff, demonstrating good customer service and helping out when the store was slammed with business.

They ignored my advice and opened the business with borrowed money. Eighteen months later they were struggling, barely breaking even, working at the store every day and dreading each new scoop of ice cream. Unfortunately, debt kept them tied to the ice cream parlor. Closing down was not an option.
Bill and Sue had allowed their emotions and dreams of a successful business to overshadow their decision. If they had looked closer they would have discovered a passion God had already placed

within them. Both were in professions where counseling skills were needed. Instead of an ice cream store, they should have pursued a business where their counseling abilities would be key.

Passion gives us the energy and desire to press on during difficult times. Christ, speaking to the church at Laodicea, said, *"So because you are lukewarm, and neither hot nor cold, I will spit you out of My mouth"* (Revelation 3:16, NASB). We cannot effectively serve God if we are lukewarm in our devotion to Him and likewise we cannot effectively work in a business where we have little passion.

God places a passion in our hearts that must come from Him and Him alone.

Establish A Clear Mission

Successful business owners establish a mission with a clear vision for their business. Just as a painter must "see" the finished masterpiece before paint is ever put to canvas, an entrepreneur must "see" into the future and determine, with God's direction, what their business will look like. Prayerfully gaining vision and establishing a mission provide a critical foundation for any business success.

Scripture relates, *"Where there is no vision, the people perish"* (Proverbs 29:18a, KJV), or as the New Living Translation states, *"When people do not accept divine guidance, they run wild."* A clear vision and mission will keep your business on track, while muddied vision will cause your business to follow unrelated rabbit trails, to drift off course, and to ultimately fail.

The apostle Paul writes, *"I press on toward the goal for the prize of the upward call of God in Christ Jesus"* (Philippians 3:14, NASB). Following Paul's example, we need to keep our mind on the prize of Christ and keep our eyes on our business mission.
The Mission Statement

Every business, large or small, needs a well-developed mission statement. The mission needs to state, in one or two sentences, why you exist, and what you do well that others do poorly or cannot do at all. Penning a catchy mission statement and then sticking it in a drawer or framing it on your wall without referring back to it will not work. You must keep your mission in mind, allowing it to shape your focus and keep you on a defined path of developing and maintaining your business.

• Staying on mission

A plant nursery in Flagstaff, Arizona has the following mission: "To comprehensively grow native plant species of Northern Arizona that will enhance the yards and properties of customers." That simple mission keeps the nursery on track. Often, they have been tempted to carry non-native flowers and plants, but they quickly realized those products are outside their mission.

Communicating your business vision to your customers is also important. The nursery, for example, uses every opportunity to advertise the fact that they carry the largest selection of native plant materials in Arizona. They advertise that their plants need low water and are able to withstand the cold winters, abundant sun, and periodic drought conditions. Customers become accustomed to going there first when looking for locally produced plants.

The nursery's clear vision helps focus the business, along with each employee and their customers, on what the business does well: providing a good selection of native plants. Other nurseries in the area do not have the experience or room to grow the native plants. Instead, they purchase plants from wholesalers, which may not be as well suited for the climate.

By closely following their mission, the owner, staff, and customers know what to expect from the business. Their expectation matches what the business can deliver.

• Getting off track

Not paying attention to your mission can bring you a lot of heartache and cost you a great deal of money!

IBM decided to expand into the telecommunications business instead of staying exclusively in the computer business. IBM lost millions of dollars in a joint venture with PBX systems in Europe. It then took another beating by owning stock in MCI (it sold that same stock at a loss before MCI took off). Then IBM lost again in a joint venture with Mitel. Finally, IBM lost over a billion dollars in an investment with Rolm Telecommunications. IBM lost sight of their original mission: to innovate, manufacture, and service computer systems.

Good Works ... The Final Step

There are many people who enjoy the enthusiasm of prayer, developing a dream or vision, and believing God for His blessings. Dreaming is easy! But there is an additional step that is necessary for success. James 2:17 states, *"Faith by itself, if it is not accompanied by action, is dead"* (NIV). In other words, we must be willing to add consistent good works to our faith. We must be willing to bear the cost.

Most of the time our vision will be accomplished over time, not overnight. Our long-term commitment and focus on our mission along with consistent good works will allow us, like a painter, to create the final product we desire.

God wants you to succeed. He has a plan for your life, a plan for good and not for evil. He desires that you will seek His will, understand His timing, pursue your passion, establish a clear and unwavering mission, and stay strong in His strength to accomplish all that He has ordained for your life.

If you are just beginning in your business life, then you will be well served to operate in God's orderly process right from the start. If you have already experienced a failure because you did not know or did not follow these principles, then you can be assured that God wishes to redeem your past. He is a gracious God, full of love, new life, and fresh beginnings!

CONSIDER:

• Have you chosen your cornerstone?

• Have you prayerfully established your mission statement?

• These are vitally important decisions to make BEFORE taking the next step.

ACTION STEPS:

1. Write out your mission statement. It should explain why your business exists.

2. Does your mission statement state what you can do well?

ROADMAP SIGNAL:

STOP: I can't write out a statement at this time.

WAIT: I have a mission, but am unclear what I can do well that others can't do.

GO: I have written out a mission statement that states why the business exists and what can be done well.

CHAPTER 2

Laying Your Cornerstone

Adam wanted to open an auto repair business. He had 15 years experience working with an automotive dealership and then an independent garage. He started to pray and plan about how he would open his own business. Adam was clear about his mission: to become the premier mechanic of high performance and racing cars in the city.

He worked out a financial plan, calculating he needed $80,000 to start the business. Adam had $25,000 in savings and a home that he shared with his wife, Emma, valued at $220,000 with a $155,000 first mortgage. He figured he could borrow an additional $85,000 on the house. That combined with a 110% second loan and the $25,000 savings would give him a total of $110,000; plenty Adam figured to give him the needed start.

Adam looked for a garage location and selected an excellent spot that needed some work and zoning approval from the city. He agreed to rent the space subject to city approval and some upgrading of the building done by the landlord.

However, his wife, Emma, was unsettled about taking on the debt and the increased mortgage on the home. Both Emma and Adam continued to pray for God's will to be revealed. Meanwhile, Adam kept his current job while preparing to strike out on his own.

At his local church Adam met Carter, a man who ran a very successful business. Carter offered to review Alan's business plan and offer some experienced advice. Carter was concerned that Adam may have trouble building up the business before his cash reserve ran out in four months.

While Adam pondered Carter's advice and Emma's concerns, the landlord called and reported that the city zoning board refused to grant the exception and he was unable to rent the building for the repair shop. Adam could have continued to plunge ahead, but given the zoning denial, Emma's unease, and Carter's advice, he accepted all this as God's providential check on the venture, at least for a time.

Nine months later Adam's uncle died and left him an inheritance of $75,000 that would be paid within six months time. Soon after Adam received the news, the owner of the shop where Adam worked came to him and explained he wanted to retire and sell the business. He asked Adam if he was interested in buying it. The price was $150,000 for everything, including equipment.

By this time, Adam and Emma had saved another $15,000 to add to their previous savings; together with their inheritance, they had a grand total of $115,000. The owner agreed to accept $100,000 down, with payments for the $50,000 over a two-year period.

Because the existing business was already profitable, it would not be consuming cash. That would not have been the case with his original plan of starting from scratch. Also, no second mortgage was required on the home. Emma was enthusiastic and Carter endorsed the new plan.

Adam was able to obtain an established business with a positive cash flow for $50,000 in total debt rather than the $85,000 second mortgage. Within fifteen months, Adam and Emma owned the business free and clear.

Had they moved forward with the first plan, they would have faced a likely business failure and the loss of their home. The Lord already had a plan, *a plan for Adam's welfare* and best interests, and by waiting for God's perfect timing, Adam received God's blessing.

God's Process

The Lord has established a process, a Holy process for any earthly endeavor. *"Therefore thus says the Lord GOD, 'Behold, I am laying in Zion a stone, a tested stone, a costly cornerstone for the foundation, firmly placed. He who believes in it will not be disturbed'"* (Isaiah 28:16, NASB).

When we work God's plan, we will be guided to fulfill His perfect will. That process includes:

1. Having a right relationship with God

2. Being sensitive to God's providence

3. Listening to God's Helper

4. Using God's Word as our guide

5. Operating according to His time schedule

6. Co-laboring with God

7. Obtaining wise counsel

#1 Right Relationship with God

Our first and foremost responsibility is to honor God in everything we do. Paul confirmed this in 1 Corinthians 10:31 when he wrote, *"So whether you eat or drink or whatever you do, do it all for the glory of God"* (NIV). Jesus taught, *"But seek first His kingdom and His righteousness; and all these things shall be added to you"* (Matthew 6:33, NASB).

Our relationship with the Lord must be on solid footing. Any unconfessed sin in our lives will block the empowerment of God and the Holy Spirit in our endeavor.

If our top priority is to merely seek business success, then God cannot bless us. Our focus must be on our eternal relationship first. If you are unsure of your relationship with God, please turn to page 193.

#2 God's Providence

In our enthusiasm we may want to charge forth and do our own thing. We can often believe a good work or noble endeavor must be God's perfect will, but that is not always the case. For example, when the Apostle Paul was on a mission trip he was forbidden to speak in Asia and instead was instructed by the Holy Spirit to travel to Bithynia (See Acts 16:6-7). Later, Paul received a clear vision from the Holy Spirit to go to Macedonia (see Acts 16:9-10).

Why Paul would be blocked from preaching the Gospel in one location is a mystery, but God had a plan for Paul and closed one door while opening another.

#3 God's Helper

Jesus promised we would not be alone; He would send us a Helper. *"But the Helper, the Holy Spirit, whom the Father will send in my name, He will teach you all things"* (John 14:26, NKJV).

The Apostle Paul also referred to this Helper when he wrote, *"But God has revealed it to us by his Spirit. The Spirit searches all things, even the deep things of God"* (1 Corinthians 2:10, NIV). Since Jesus referred to the Holy Spirit as the helper, we need to seek and listen to the Helper whether we are starting a business or doing any other endeavor.

#4 God's Word

The Scriptures include guidance for every aspect of our lives. The Lord, speaking through Isaiah said, *"So shall my word be that goes forth from my mouth; It shall not return to me empty, without accomplishing what I desire, and without succeeding in the matter for which it was sent"* (Isaiah 55:11, NASB).

As we move forward, we need to evaluate every step we take in the light of God's Word, seeking His direction. Whenever we see that our thoughts, direction, or actions are contrary to God's Word, we need to stop and re-examine our situation.

The truth is we cannot honor God in only part of what we do. We must honor Him in everything. Some businesses are obviously illegal while others may be legal but still dishonor the Lord, like a bookstore that sells pornography. Some retail franchises even require a store to carry pornographic magazines. This type of franchise would be a poor choice if you desire God's help and blessing.

The Apostle Peter cautioned us, *"As obedient children, do not be conformed to the former lusts which were yours in your ignorance, but like the Holy One who called you, be holy yourselves also in all your behavior"* (1 Peter 1:14-15, NASB).

A used car lot owner told me that if he were totally honest with every buyer, the business would collapse. If violating God's Word by being untruthful with customers is the only way to stay in business, then you are in a business that is dishonoring to God—and you need to walk away.

#5 God's Timing

We often say that "timing is everything" and the Word of God certainly agrees. The prophet Habakkuk wrote, *"For the vision is yet for the appointed time; it hastens toward the goal, and it will not fail. Though it tarries, wait for it; for it will certainly come, it will not delay"* (Habakkuk 2:3, NASB).

Being patient to discern and trust God's timing will spare us unnecessary frustration and failure.

As Adam and Emma learned by being obedient, God had a plan for Adam to open his own repair shop. But the Lord delayed the plan for a good reason, and that delay became a tremendous blessing.

#6 Co-Laboring with God

We were not meant to do things in our own strength. The Lord wants to be our total resource in every endeavor. As King Solomon wrote, *"Unless the LORD builds the house, those who build it labor in vain. Unless the LORD guards the city, the guard keeps watch in vain"* (Psalm 127:1, NRSV).

By inviting the Lord to become our "senior partner," we will not labor in vain.

#7 Obtaining Wise Counsel

One of the most important steps of any business is that of obtaining, utilizing, and acting on the wise counsel of others.

Scripture provides a clear picture of the need for counsel. *"Where there is no guidance, the people fall, but in abundance of counselors there is victory"* (Proverbs 11:14, NASB), and, *"Without consultation plans are frustrated"* (Proverbs 15:22, NASB).

We have a tendency to not want to seek and follow counsel, but King Solomon taught, *"The way of the fool is right in his own eyes, but a wise man is he who listens to counsel"* (Proverbs 12:15, NASB).

We can become impatient, not wanting to wait and seek advice from others. Invariably, when we seek counsel, we are asked questions – tough questions that we may have difficulty answering. The very process of thinking through responses to tough questions will help clarify our thinking and help us form a more effective plan.

In our humanness we seem to have a rebellious streak. God spoke to Isaiah saying, *"I have spread out my hands all day long to a rebellious people, who walk in the way which is not good, following their own thoughts"* (Isaiah 65:2, NASB).

Also, given our natural drive for accomplishment, we entrepreneurs are especially prone to going our own way. We need to balance our drive with the wisdom of utilizing Godly counsel.

Counselors You Can Trust

Not all counselors are created equal. Be mindful of that as you look for advice. The first criteria for any counselor you choose is obvious: godliness. David wrote, *"The mouth of the righteous utters wisdom, and his tongue speaks justice. The law of his God is in his heart; His steps do not slip"* (Psalm 37:30-31, NASB).

Seek advise from select individuals who have a strong walk with the Lord that is clearly demonstrated in their lives. Consider the following counselors and whom you could utilize in your particular situation:

• Counsel from your spouse

If you are married, the first and foremost counselor is your spouse. Whether it is the husband or the wife or both who start a business, the spouse is still the best counselor.

Spouses tend to be the vehicle God uses to communicate clearly and directly to us. Wives especially tend to have an innate sense that can be uncannily accurate, regardless of the amount of business training or knowledge they possess. A husband or wife who steps out against counsel and takes risks which make the spouse uncomfortable is usually headed for disaster.

Asking your spouse for advice and counsel is a way to show honor and respect. It is a way of saying, "I love you. I need your help." Furthermore, making decisions together will help maintain your relationship when difficult times come, as they will in any business.

Even if the venture turns sour, your relationship will persevere because you made the decisions together. If the husband or wife makes a unilateral decision, then the other may feel like an "outsider," and ultimately grow resentful.

Just as God created Eve as a wife and helpmate for Adam (Genesis 2:18), so our spouse is designed to be a helper in any business endeavor, not a hindrance. When Jacob was considering departing from his father-in-law's land, he consulted with his wives before making the decision to depart (See Genesis 31:4-16).

Moving forward without the agreement of your spouse is unwise and contrary to God's Word. Decide that you will never embark on a venture without your spouse's informed consent and agreement.

• Counsel from family

Seeking counsel from certain family members who know you well in another way to ensure your success. They have seen you function is a wide spectrum of life's circumstances and can offer valuable feedback about your strengths and weaknesses.

Obviously, use judgment here. Not every family member can offer you wise advice. Be selective in your choice of counselors.

King Solomon instructed, *"My son, observe the commandment of your father"* (Proverbs 6:20a, NASB). Thoroughly discussing any venture with family members can give powerful insights, as long as you give them permission to be candid and avoid being defensive.

Outlining your plan, identifying the strengths needed for success in your particular business, and then asking for their feedback is the best approach. However, do not allow family members to carry more influence or weight than your spouse.

• Counsel from friends

If you have one or more close friends who know you pretty well, you could make them part of your counseling team. Make sure the friends you select have generally demonstrated both wisdom and success in their personal decision-making. King Solomon affirmed making the right selection of counselors when he wrote, *"He who walks with the wise grows wise, but a companion of fools suffers harm"* (Proverbs 13:20, NIV).

Don was a great software engineer. His work was described as brilliant and he received outstanding evaluations along with financial raises from his employer. Don had a strong desire to develop his own business and planned to hire a small team of experts to assist him. He strongly believed that clients would quickly gravitate to his business.

While it was true that Don was a brilliant and creative software engineer, he was not an effective communicator. Everyone close to Don could see it, which was why as an employee other colleagues "filled in the gaps" for Don in the communication area.

Both Don's wife and his close friends felt Don would not do well in a business of his own due to his poor communication skills. However, Don plunged ahead against the advice of his wife and friends.

Ten months later, and $40,000 poorer, Don had to close his business and go to work for another software development company. He could have saved himself, his family, and his friends a lot of grief and heartache by listening to their concerns.

It was not that his wife and friends possessed more business experience than Don. They might not have even known 10% of what Don did about software development. What they did know, on the other hand, was Don himself—and that was key!

• Counsel from business associates

Obtaining wisdom and counsel from fellow businesspeople who have already walked the path of your current interests can provide you with powerful and timely advice. People with general business experience can also be helpful, but someone with specific experience is ideal.

Share your vision and general plans and then ask for input and guidance. Make it clear that you do not want them to be polite and just "bless" your plans. You want sincere feedback and advice.

• Counsel from an attorney

In today's litigious society and with the legal requirements of running any business, legal counsel is a necessity for everyone in business. Even if you have a simple business structure and do not see any outstanding issues, establishing a relationship with an attorney is important.

For example, your lawyer can read a lease document to ensure that you understand the fine print. Also, should you get sued or encounter any other legal problem, already having a legal relationship will prevent you from scrambling about at the last minute for advice or making the wrong decision for lack of good counsel.

NOTE: When hiring professional counselors, obtain and check references.

• Counsel from a banker

Even a simple business requires a banking relationship, even if you just have a checking account. Start with an appointment with a bank manager and explain your business and what services you expect to use.

Generally, the more accounts you have (both business and personal) with one bank, the more valuable a customer you become and the more helpful management will be to keep your business. In addition, a bank manager may be able to give you suggestions for better services that will save you time and money. Most banks have special packages for small businesses. Take the time to shop several banks and look for the best deal and personal relationship available.

• Counsel from an insurance agent

All businesses require insurance to protect your business investment. A competent insurance agent can help you explore the coverage that fits your needs at a cost you can afford. Searching the Internet for the best rate may be great for car insurance, but for comprehensive business insurance, a hands-on agent is best.

Your personal agent can advise you on the best way to secure your property from theft and fire, thus protecting your assets and reducing your financial risk. The agent can also suggest liability insurance based on the safe keeping of your particular products or services.

• Counsel from "special needs" people

Depending on how specialized your field, you may from time to time need to seek counsel from a "special needs" list of people. For example, an experienced advertising veteran can be of great assistance when opening an independent agency.

Carole was opening a Human Resources consulting business after a successful 20-year corporate career. By seeking advertising counsel from people in different cities that had opened branches of their own, she obtained valuable information to assist in making the change to personal ownership.

CONSIDER:

• While seeking the wise counsel of others is certainly a biblical principle and even a mandate, the Lord must always remain your #1 counselor as you go forward.

• God promises, *"I will instruct you and teach you in the way which you should go; I will counsel you with my eye upon you"* (Psalm 32:8).

ACTION STEPS:

1. Create a list of counselors.

2. Contact each and determine if every person is willing to assume that role.

3. Write out steps 1 through 7 and document how the Lord is leading you through each item.

ROADMAP SIGNAL:

STOP: I have no counselors.

WAIT: I have a list of possible counselors, but have not yet asked for help.

GO: I have prepared a list of counselors, and they have agreed to help me.

CHAPTER 3

Assessing Yourself Personally

This will help you determine whether starting a business at this time is a good decision. The assessment inventories discussed in this section are designed to guide you through an honest and careful evaluation of your readiness.

Start the evaluation process by committing your plans to God in prayer. As you place your dreams of ownership on the altar before the Lord, be prepared for Him to answer, "Yes," "No," or "Wait." If you will allow the Lord to open or close the doors, rather than kicking them down yourself, your chance of success will markedly improve.

If you become caught up in the enthusiasm of starting a business and neglect an orderly process of evaluation, it will ultimately cause you heartache, not joy. The psalm that says, *"Unless the LORD builds the house, those who build it labor in vain"* (Psalm 127:1, NRSV), applies to building a business as well as a home.

Assessment: Marriage & Family Considerations

Founding a new business is a challenging endeavor that will demand a commitment of time, energy, and focus; and, the full support of your family. Often, our passion to start a business overshadows the importance of our family relationships. However, the Lord makes it clear that our priorities are to be the Lord first (Matthew 6:33), our family next (1 Timothy 5:8), and our work or business last (Ecclesiastes 3:13).

Genuine "buy-in" and support from your family is essential for business success. The entire family will be involved with a new business venture, either by working or supporting you. *If you are married, your most loyal support will often come from your spouse.*

Counting the cost as a family is a key step in the evaluation process. As your plans unfold, keep your family members up to date and let them know what you are thinking. Above all, avoid surprises.

If you are married, take this marriage health inventory test. On a scale of 1-to-10, measure yourself and then honestly evaluate your score. Write your score on the grid to the right:

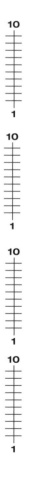

How well do I communicate with my spouse?
Do I spend time with my spouse, catching her/him up to date with my day, plans, spending, dreams, etc? (Though one of you might run the business exclusively, the other needs to know what is going on to a certain degree.)

How often do we pray together?
Is praying together important to my spouse, our marriage relationship, our family, and me? Are we open to praying aloud together? Do we pray together as much as I would like?

Are we on the same page?
Does my spouse know what I am doing or wanting to do? Are we aware financially, emotionally, and mentally of what is required to successfully launch this business? Are we both on the same page in areas that matter most?

Do we share the same financial values and limitations?
Are we in agreement on spending habits, spending limits, and borrowing money? Have we communicated how much financial risk we are willing to take to reach our dreams? Is one of us willing to take greater risks than the other—and is the non-risk-taker at peace with the decision?

Are our boundaries in place?

Have we discussed what is required, especially from the time and money side of things? How much time are we willing to spend each week? How much money are we willing or able to spend overall? Are our safeguards in place?

Are we spending enough time together?

Do I wait for my spouse to suggest time away on a date? Do we spend regularly scheduled time together without distractions? (This counts time away with your children, if you have children. Family time is separate and also important.)

Am I an open book?

Am I defensive when my spouse asks about my business dealings? Does my spouse even have the freedom to ask me things? (Running a business involves transparency, which is to your direct benefit!)

Do we believe in each other?

Does my spouse believe in me and do I believe in my spouse? Regardless of what I do and regardless of who brings home more money, it is vitally important that we believe (verbally express it!) in each other. Do I express my belief in my spouse?

How quick am I to forgive?

Issues will arise; that is just natural, but am I quick to seek forgiveness and to extend forgiveness? Do I sleep regularly on the couch because of arguments? If so, am I willing to right the wrongs before going to bed?

Am I a good listener?

How well do I listen to my spouse's ideas, thoughts, corrections, and recommendations? (Do you "connect" with what is being said, implied, and meant? Listen as you would like to be listened to!)

SECTION 2: Evaluating Your Options

What was your average score? If this quick survey shows that your marriage needs work, focus your time and energy on strengthening your marriage before starting a new business.

Many people believe that the excitement and challenge of a new undertaking will ease their marriage problems, but the strain of starting a new business will only increase the pressure on your personal life, often past the breaking point.

Assessment: Financial Considerations

To "count the cost" financially, take an inventory of your net worth in the following manner:

1. In the following form, value your assets conservatively:

ASSETS (present market value)	
Cash on hand / checking account	_____
Savings	_____
Stocks and bonds	_____
Cash value of life insurance	_____
Coins	_____
Home	_____
Other real estate	_____
Mortgges / notes receivable	_____
Business valuation	_____
Automobiles	_____
Furniture	_____
Jewelry	_____
Other personal property	_____
IRA	_____
Pension / retirement plan	_____
Other assets	_____
TOTAL ASSETS:	_____

2. In the following form, value your liabilities:

LIABILITIES (current amount owed)

Current bills	_____
Credit card debt	_____
Automobile loans	_____
Home mortgage	_____
Other real estate mortgages	_____
Personal debts to relatives	_____
Business loans	_____
Educational loans	_____
Medical bills	_____
Life insurance loans	_____
Bank loans	_____
Student loans	_____
Other debts and loans	_____
TOTAL LIABILITIES:	_____

3. Compare your assets to your liabilities to see where you are financially:

TOTAL ASSETS	_____
– TOTAL LIABILITIES	_____
= NET WORTH	_____

Once you have determined your net worth, you will have a better idea of how much cash you have available to purchase or start up a business. Most businesses will require some kind of cash investment. Buying a business, even on credit, usually requires a minimum of a 30% down payment. Not only will starting a new business require cash for a variety of start-up expenses, you can usually expect to have an operating deficit for one to three years before your business becomes profitable.

SECTION 2: Evaluating Your Options

If you have a negative net worth, you are not prepared financially to start a business.

> **Lack of available cash is the number one reason for start-up failure.**

You will not have the money you need to invest in a business or fund the necessary start-up costs. Lack of available cash is the number one reason for start-up failure. Interpret a cash shortfall as an answer from the Lord ("no" or "wait"), plain and simple.

If you are short of cash, consider the possibility of starting your business as a part-time venture, or simply continue to plan and save. But remember that at some point, every business will require a cash investment.

In addition to calculating your net worth, you should know your personal budget. How much monthly income is required to meet your family's needs? This number is vitally important!

Use the worksheets on the following pages to calculate your personal budget.

MONTHLY INCOME & EXPENSES

STEP #1: Calculate your GROSS Income / Month:

    Salary   _____

    Interest   _____

    Dividends   _____

    Other   _____

TOTAL INCOME: _____

STEP #2: Subtract:

    Tithe   _____

    Tax (Includes Fed, State, FICA, etc.)   _____

TOTAL DEDUCTIONS: _____

STEP #3: This leaves your

  NET SPENDABLE INCOME: _____

STEP #4: Calculate your total expenses:

    HOUSING: _____

      Mortgage / Rent   _____

      Insurance   _____

      Taxes   _____

      Electricity   _____

      Gas   _____

      Water   _____

      Sanitation   _____

      Telephone   _____

      Internet   _____

      Maintenance   _____

      Other   _____

    FOOD: _____

MONTHLY INCOME & EXPENSES continued

AUTOMOBILE: _____
  Payments _____
  Gas & Oil _____
  Insurance / License _____
  Taxes _____
  Maint / Repair _____

INSURANCE: _____
  Life _____
  Medical _____
  Other _____

DEBTS: _____
  Credit Card _____
  Loans / notes _____
  Other _____

SAVINGS: _____

ENTERTAINMENT / RECREATION: _____
  Eating out _____
  Baby sitters _____
  Activities _____
  Vacations _____
  Other _____

MEDICAL EXPENSES: _____
  Doctor _____
  Dentist _____
  Drugs _____
  Other _____

SCHOOL / CHILD CARE: _____
   Tuition _____
   Materials _____
   Transportation _____
   Day care _____

MISC: _____
   Toiletry / cosmetics _____
   Beauty / barber _____
   Laundry / cleaning _____
   Magazines / newspapers _____
   Allowances _____
   Cash _____
   Other _____

INVESTMENTS: _____

TOTAL EXPENSES: _____

STEP #5: **NET INCOME:** _____
   minus **EXPENSES:** _____
   equals **SURPLUS INCOME:** _____

STEP #6:
   Put surplus income in an allocated category.

If you have difficulty maintaining a personal budget, you may also have trouble setting and keeping a business budget.

During the start-up stages of your business, you may have to cut certain items from your family budget. Be careful not to cut back too much or you will place undue hardship on the rest of the family.

Key Question: What are the consequences of possible business failure: personally, financially, and for my family?

Optimistic entrepreneurs often do not want to consider the possibility of failure. But no matter how much experience, skill, and money you have to invest in a new business, do not fail to plan for the possibility that the business could fail. Clearly understanding where you stand financially and with your family relationships will help you evaluate your decision. For example, a married couple in their early thirties without children can assume a far greater risk than a father of six young children or a person nearing retirement.

ASK YOURSELF:

- What is your net worth? Write it here: _____

- Do you have a budget?

- Are you on budget or over budget?

- What can you do to change that?

Assessment: Personal Goals

Establishing personal goals in life is important for any individual. The most successful and satisfying businesses are those that come closest to satisfying the owner's personal goals. Many people like the possibility of earning more money, improving their lifestyle, being their own boss, becoming more creative, establishing a retirement plan, picking their own hours, and so on.

As you evaluate your goals, remember that God owns everything (Psalm 24:1). Becoming a business owner is simply one way of practicing stewardship of God's property. Furthermore, we are called to honor God in everything we do (1 Corinthians 10:31). A business is not an end in itself, but rather a means to accomplish your personal, God-given vision.

Take a moment to write down the top three things that you believe starting a business will accomplish in your life:

1. _____

2. _____

3. _____

For instance, if it will increase your income, write it down. If it will provide you with the freedom to take care of your family, write that down. Whatever it is that motivates you to take action, that is what you want to record.

There are no right or wrong answers, only honest answers. Your properly directed motivation will help carry you through the inevitable tough times that every entrepreneur faces.

Key Question: Can my motivation for starting a business be satisfied in any other way? Should it be satisfied in another way?

A few years ago, the owners (husband and wife) of a travel agency that was losing money came to me for advice. They were struggling to meet current bills and becoming increasingly nervous because of the financial pressure. I asked why, at age 55, they had decided to open a travel agency. They said they loved the travel business, thought they could manage it part-time, and wanted to be able to enjoy inexpensive travel. I helped them close down their business

SECTION 2: Evaluating Your Options

and obtain part-time positions with a larger agency, which enabled them to stay connected to the travel industry, do their own traveling, and provide firsthand feedback to their clients. They discovered that their vision could easily be achieved without the challenges of owning a business.

Consider Bill. He had an interest in rare coins and was thinking seriously about quitting his job as an engineer to pursue his passion. Although he had been an astute collector for many years, he lacked the business acumen to become a coin dealer. Instead, Bill restructured his job and became a contract engineer, reducing his work time commitment. He then started working part-time for a local coin dealer. The interaction with other collectors satisfied his passion for being involved in the coin market, while the combined income of his two jobs preserved his regular cash flow and allowed him to continue to meet the needs of his family.

In both of these examples, there was a creative way to accomplish the goal without putting undue stress on the family finances.

Another common reason for starting a business is to "fire the boss." Maybe you are great at what you do and you know that if the boss would just get out of the way, you could be a lot more productive, serve customers better, and get things done more efficiently. Not only that, but if you owned your own business, you could pursue your vision of a business owner's lifestyle: accumulating wealth, having more leisure time, and having the freedom to do what you think is right.

If your sole motivation is to "fire the boss" and start your own business, you will soon find that you have *many* bosses (Customers, Accounts Receivable, Accounts Payable, Payroll, OSHA, the IRS, just to name a few) clamoring for your attention.

You may be able to accomplish your goals by changing jobs, getting more education, developing an extracurricular interest into a side business, focusing more free time into your current hobby, or taking other action.

Ask yourself if you would stay in your current job provided you received a 20 or 30 percent raise? If so, consider the wisdom of not starting a business, but working at becoming more valuable to your present employer (or another employer) before taking on the risks and stress of starting your first business. Ask your counselors to validate your motivation and whether starting a venture is the best way to meet your personal goals.

ASK YOURSELF:

• Do you have a very clear reason for wanting to start your business?

• Do you have a reason why that will motivate you to take action day after day?

• Have you taken and scored your personal assessment?

• Have you validated the feedback recieved from your counselors?

• Have you documented your personal finances?

Assessment: Personal Qualities Inventory

Each person has gifts and talents provided by God. Take stock of your unique combination of personal gifts by answering the questions listed below. They will help you determine how the qualities you possess match up with the qualities you need to succeed in your own business.

Score yourself on each question (as you are today, not as you see yourself in the future) using a scale of 1-to-10, with "1" representing you possess no qualities to fill the need and "10" representing you have all the qualities necessary. Be honest in your personal assessment.

Do I have a passion for the business?

10

1

Over time, the day in, day out grind of any job or business will dull your interest. That is when you will need to rely on your God-given passion for your business to keep your interest alive. A bakery owner has to love handling the dough, the feel of a perfectly kneaded loaf, the smell of the ovens, and the smiles and hungry looks from customers. The owner of the ice cream shop must love ice cream, must care about butterfat content and optimum "mouth feel" of a well-made batch, and must enjoy the delight of kids (of all ages!) as they peer through the glass and select their favorite flavor.

If a business plan looks like a good deal but fails to ignite your passion, STOP! If a business opportunity is right for you, you will feel your excitement grow and your blood begin to flow a little warmer in your veins.

Am I familiar with the business and the industry?

10

1

Understanding a business before you start is a significant advantage. You could probably learn any business, but the lessons are often painful and expensive. When rating yourself in this area, consider your knowledge of the entire business, not just one or two parts of it. A great chef may have an outstanding knowledge of food preparation, menu items, and kitchen efficiency, but lack the necessary knowledge about selecting locations, menu pricing, dining trends, or determining the best floor plan. Certainly, you can consult with others or hire expertise in areas where you are not as strong, but the more knowledge you have about your proposed business and its industry, the easier it will be for you to manage the operation successfully.

Do I understand the nuts and bolts of the business?

10

1

This is the flip side to the question above. Understanding the nuts and bolts of a business is different from understanding the overall business. A car wash owner may understand location selection, marketing, hiring, and managing staff, but not understand the mechanical aspects of the equipment. The owner would need to commit to learning the ins and outs of the mechanical system or make sure that another staff member has the necessary expertise. Also, every business at some point boils down to customer service. A successful owner will understand the nuts and bolts in this area as well.

Do I have effective people skills?

A business owner must be able to communicate effectively with employees, suppliers, service people, salespeople, and most importantly, the customers. The ability to get along with others, the capacity to empathize and to understand their needs is critical. A good barometer of your people skills is your ability to demonstrate respect for others and earn their respect in return.

Do I express myself effectively?

Business owners must be able to effectively communicate a vision for their business and sell their products and services to customers. When ordering products or supplies, an owner must communicate well with vendors to ensure timely delivery of the necessary inventory. Effective leaders develop the ability to influence others with clear, persuasive arguments.

Do I possess good listening skills?

The ability to listen, and listen well, is also important. Successful business owners know how to listen to their customers and employees. Employees are often the source of great cost-saving ideas and innovations. Listening to your customers will give you an inside track on the competition when it comes to meeting your customer's needs.

Am I a motivated self-starter?

With no "boss" other than your customers and the business itself, an owner must possess a strong motivation to succeed and have a built-in drive to achieve needed goals. Owners who arrive "on time" rather than early, who sit back when business is slow, or struggle to get going on key projects, are destined for difficulty. Effective owners welcome every day

as a new challenge and plunge into their projects like a kid diving into a pool. They are leaders.

Do I consistently follow through?

10

Follow-through is simply finishing what you have started. A few completed projects are better than dozens of great ideas left undone. World-class customer service requires many interlocking steps. For example, taking a customer's order may involve answering the phone, taking down accurate

1

information, packing and shipping the product, billing the customer, and collecting the bill when due. Failure to follow through at any of these junctures could mean losing a sale, a customer—or everything.

Do I have effective organization skills and do I pay attention to details?

10

Details, details, details can drive some people nuts. In business, however, attention to detail may be the difference between success and failure. Some business owners spend literally hours each week looking for lost papers or notes on their desk, time that would be much better spent building the

1

business. Accounting, inventory control, and other important aspects of business operations require strict attention to detail. God is a God of order, not disorder, and part of our mandate here on earth is to bring order out of chaos (Genesis 1:28-30). Your current workplace, kitchen, or garage is a good barometer of your organizational skills

Do I make decisive and prompt decisions?

10

Decisions are part of a business owner's daily routine. The ability to make good and timely decisions is a crucial skill. Some owners agonize over issues such as whether to make eight photocopies or ten, wasting time and energy on irrelevant decisions. Owners must be comfortable making

1

decisions because they will be called on regularly to decide such things as whether to accept a customer return, whether to give an employee an extra day off, and when to order more inventory. Some decisions will require more time,

Text in left margin:

information, or consultation than others, but most can and should be made quickly.

Do I maintain my personal integrity in all circumstances?

Businesses of all sizes, from Enron to the tiniest restaurant, have collapsed because of a failure to adhere to ethical biblical standards. A restaurant owner who ignores inconvenient health department rules may be closed down by a surprise inspection. A hardware store owner who ignores repeated fire department citations could lose everything when the business burns down. Many businesses with cash-flow problems fall behind on their tax payments, and the owner ends up paying fines or going to jail. Without supervision or accountability, an owner with marginal integrity is likely to fall quickly. If you are one whose promises tend to be broken, you will struggle in building a strong bond of trust with your customers and employees.

Do I effectively solve problems?

Every business produces a steady stream of challenges and problems to be solved—and the buck stops with the owner. The ability to identify quickly what is going wrong, understand why, and then determine a solution is paramount to business success. Problems left unresolved will grow larger and be joined by more problems along the way. Effective problem-solvers look at each new challenge as an opportunity to improve the business, not as just another aggravation.

Am I resilient?

Every business owner will have challenging days and downright disastrous days. Eventually you will lose an important customer or great employee; you will experience bad debts or work through cash-flow problems of your own. Business owners cannot allow themselves to become downtrodden. They must pick themselves up and move on —enthusiastically! A sourpuss owner inspires no one.

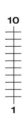

SECTION 2: Evaluating Your Options

Do I repeat mistakes?

10

1

We all make mistakes and hope to learn from them, but some business owners pay dearly for each new lesson. It is important to learn to view mistakes as learning opportunities, to understand what went wrong and why, and then grow from the experience. Do you implement changes to avoid repeating the same mistakes? When your furnace goes out during January, will you start having it serviced regularly in October, or will you wait for another midwinter breakdown?

Do I have high work quality standards?

10

1

Superb quality and customer service is a hallmark of all successful organizations. A passion for delivering the best possible products and service is vital. In your current position, do you have a passion for quality? When working around the house, are your jobs neat, well done, and completed?

Do I have a "passionate personality"?

10

1

The owner is the number one ambassador for the business. Who will be enthusiastic about your business and demonstrate that enthusiasm to your employees and customers if not you? Your passion will attract customers and good employees. Some owners care deeply about their business, but unless they express that passion through their personality and attitude, they will fail to excite others.

What is my risk-taking temperament?

10

1

Given the failure rate for new businesses, a new owner must be able to tolerate risk. With careful planning and effective execution you can improve your likelihood for success, but risk will always be part of the equation. If you are already losing sleep over a slumping stock market or stress on the job, it will only get worse when you are at the helm of your own business.

Assessment: Personal Temperament

Different temperaments are best suited for different types of businesses. This survey will help you understand the best type of business for you.

Do I like to work by following a business model created by others?

Many successful businesspeople work better when they follow an established business model rather than creating everything from scratch. McDonald's franchise operation provides a complete business model that lays out every step of the process. McDonald's has a track record with a high percentage of successes, but franchise owners cannot deviate from the model. If you chafe under close direction, always feel a need to improve the process, and are always tinkering with your operation, do not buy a franchise.

Do I share decision making with others, or do I call all the shots?

A partnership requires giving each partner an equal say in key business decisions. If you are comfortable working with others and are happy to share decision making as well as responsibilities, a partnership may work for you. However, if you prefer to call your own shots, move forward at your own pace, and do not like to share decisions, then a partnership will create nothing but frustration and friction and will not thrive over the long haul.

Do I like to create everything from scratch?

Reinventing the wheel is usually not necessary, but some business owners prefer to create a totally new entity rather than refine or perfect an existing model. Owners who are very creative, who know what they want and exactly how everything should operate, will typically find that starting a business from scratch is the best way to go.

SECTION 2: Evaluating Your Options

Evaluating The Surveys

On all of these assessments, an average score of 4 or better on a question is considered "above average" and gives a good indication of possible business success. Scores below 3.5 indicate potential problems. If you find you are weak in one or more key aspects of the business you want to enter, BEWARE.

For example, suppose Alice the accountant struggles with being a self-starter or has trouble following through. She may be far better off working for a manager who will provide some structure and accountability. She would be frustrated, unfulfilled, and unemployed if she rushed into starting her own bookkeeping business.

> **An average score of 4 or better on a question is considered "above average" and gives a good indication of possible business success.**

Use the results of your evaluation to focus on future learning and personal discipline. The Scriptures tell us that Jesus continued to increase in wisdom—we can and should follow His example. If you see that you fall short in several key areas but still want to start a business, first shore up your weak spots and then move forward when you become better prepared.

Assignments

Assignment #1:

• List your three greatest strengths and how these relate to the business you are interested in starting.

• List your three greatest weaknesses and how these will adversely affect your business.

Assignment #2:

• Ask each of your counselors to evaluate you on each question. Do not show the counselors your personal evaluation ratings but allow them to list their own independent thoughts. Only allow them to skip a question if they truly do not know you well in that area.

• Set aside enough time to thoroughly discuss the results of the survey with your counselors, paying particular attention to questions where your ratings and their ratings differ substantially. Your objective is to obtain accurate feedback, so avoid being defensive when you hear their answers.

Do not put your counselors in the position that Paul found himself in when writing to the Galatians, "Have I now become your enemy by telling you the truth?" (Galatians 4:16, NIV). Straightforward, candid feedback (even if you do not like what you hear) is one of the most important parts of your evaluation process and one possible means by which God will show you His perfect will.

ACTION STEPS:

1. Take the personal inventory.

2. Validate with your counselors.

3. Write your key business passion, what gets you going, what creates excitement for you, and what is your motivation.

4. Write out you three greatest strengths and three greatest weaknesses.

5. Validate your strengths and weaknesses with your counselors.

SECTION 2: Evaluating Your Options

Are you satisfied with your personal profile?

- What score did your counselors give you?

- Did their scores and your scores match?

- If you were encouraged by their evaluations, that is a good sign.

- If you disagree with their results, find out why!

By this point, you have achieved a complete profile of yourself and your circumstances. Now you must listen carefully to what the Lord and godly council are saying. As God said through the prophet Jeremiah, "Call on me and I will answer you and I will tell you great things" (Jeremiah 33:3).

The Lord will answer your prayer in one of three ways:

1. **STOP:** *"It hurts you to kick against the goads"* (Acts 26:14b, NRSV).

2. **WAIT:** *"For the vision is yet for an appointed time"* (Habakkuk 2:3a, KJV).

3. **GO:** *"Arise! For this matter is your responsibility, but we will be with you; be courageous and act"* (Ezra 10:4, NASB).

A red light in any primary area—family, finances, or your personality inventory—is a sign to STOP. If you ignore the signals and plunge ahead, you are headed for disaster and future heartbreak. Pray to fully discern God's perfect will for your life, and then be obedient to follow His direction.

CHAPTER 4

Assessing Your Competition

Assessing your competition is paramount when you are considering opening a business. Deciding whether your new business will bring something unique to the market place or provide better service for an already existing niche will determine your level of success.

In Numbers 13:2, the Lord told Moses, *"Send out for yourself men so that they may spy out the land of Canaan"* (NASB). The Lord knew the people needed to understand the enemy, just as a business must understand its competition.

Evaluating the strengths and weaknesses of other businesses in the marketplace will help determine if and how you can compete. Luke 14:31 asks, *"Or what king, when he sets out to meet another king in battle, will not first sit down and take counsel whether he is strong enough with ten thousand men to encounter the one coming against him with twenty thousand?"* (NASB).

• Product Uniqueness

When scouting the competition, you need to review several key competitive factors. Begin with the basic question, "How is my product or service different from what is currently offered in the market place?"

> **Rank the uniqueness of your product.**
>
> 10 — 1

Establishing what makes you different from others is a key step in separating your business from the pack. The prophet Amos wrote, *"Does a bird fall into a trap on the ground when there is no bait in it?"* (Amos 3:5a, NASB). Your uniqueness is the "bait" needed to attract customers.

• Specialization

Rather than competing directly with an already existing business, you might consider specializing in a more specific area of the same business.

For instance, a company wishing to sell replacement windows wanted to survive in an already crowded field. They found a way to make custom colored window frames that could be marketed to decorators and high-end custom builders. By specializing and not competing "head on," they were able to remove themselves from direct competition with other window frame businesses.

A similar example is David, the shepherd boy, who faced Goliath, a nine-foot tall and well-armed giant of a man. A direct frontal attack against the giant would have been fatal. However, David was an expert at using a sling and stone and determined that by using his specialized talent he could defeat the giant. And he did.

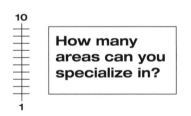

How many areas can you specialize in?

Mike and Dona wanted to open a plant nursery near Bay City, Michigan. They had the knowledge to grow and maintain plants and understood what customers wanted. However, before opening, they visited other facilities and found that numerous local stores were selling plant material below the cost they would be able to buy wholesale! While they believed they could offer better service and a higher quality of plants, they understood with the price competition so severe, developing a clientele would be difficult.

They decided to specialize in two unique markets, mature trees and garden herbs. Some homeowners wanted much larger trees than were available at current outlets. The more mature trees also needed professional handling and planting, another service the competitors did not make available. Mike and Dona had grown herbs for years, but now they grew them commercially and started advertising them in specialty catalogs and magazines.

Over time, they built up a steady and growing stream of customers wanting large trees or herb gardens. Their niche served them well. Several years after commencing operation, the business was successful. "If we had not specialized — if we had taken on the big boys directly we would never have made it," said Mike. "The best thing we did was to evaluate the competition and then determine the mission for our business. Our mission was to be the premier source of large shade and evergreen trees and the premier supplier of herb products that can be grown in the Michigan climate."

• Location, Location!

Where you actually locate your business will be a major factor in your success or failure. You certainly would not want to locate your new business too close to a strong competitor.

After careful evaluation of their competitors, a family opened a pizza takeout restaurant. Knowing that most of their customers would come from within a two-mile radius, they sought a location that was accessible, while not too close to other pizza places. The location selected was 1.5 miles from the closest competitor, and for many homes in that area, the new pizza place had now became the closest location.

> **How good is your location?**
>
> 10
> 1

In this case, the unique feature that made the restaurant successful was based on a wise selection of location.

• The Ignored Niche

Looking over the field of competitors may be daunting, but you need to look for market segments that are not well serviced. Finding an ignored niche that is not currently available can be your ticket to success.

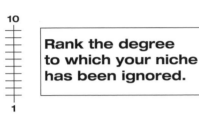

In Arizona, an auto service company wanted to expand their business. Conventional advertising brought in a few new customers, but sales were generally flat. After further study of the market, the business owner realized that the people who spoke only Spanish were not being well served.

The owner took action. He began to advertise in Spanish on Hispanic/Latino radio stations, hired customer service personnel who spoke Spanish, and even had some basic brochures and literature translated into Spanish.

The result was a 35% jump in new customers!

• Customer Service

No matter how fabulous your product or how fantastic your location, offering excellent customer service in a timely manner is a must for continued profitability. The apostle Paul elevated good service to an even higher level by offering it to the Lord. In Ephesians 6:7 he wrote, *"Render service with enthusiasm, as to the Lord and not to men and women"* (NRSV).

You will want to study the service level provided by your competitors and determine if you are capable of matching or exceeding the service offered. If you feel you can provide better service, be sure to analyze whether customers in your area of business would be willing to pay for that better service. In other words, you will need to decide if a particular type of service would be not just an effective tool to differentiate you from other similar businesses but also an added factor in your customer's buying decision.

For example, gas stations today offer very little service. We have all become accustomed to sticking in our own credit card and pumping our own gas. Paying more for gas in order to have someone pump it for us would not be a good risk. Also, most airline travelers choose their carrier based on schedule and price rather than service. In both these situations, adding more service would increase costs without necessarily attracting more customers.

In other circumstances, more available and effective customer service could be a definite drawing card. For example, I recently needed emergency service on my well pump and was told by one business that I would need to wait three weeks for a service call — which is a long time to be without water! Fortunately I was able to locate another well specialist that could fix my problem immediately, provided I paid for two hours of travel time. In this specific market, there was clearly an advantage and profitability to offering more prompt service.

> **Is your customer service the best?**
>
> 10
> —
> —
> —
> —
> —
> —
> 1

• Product Quality

In the creation story, Scripture tells us *"Then God saw everything that He had made, and indeed it was very good"* (Genesis 1:31a, NKJV). We need to ensure that the quality of our product or service is also very good. Effectively scouting the competition helps you understand the level of quality you must deliver to not only meet, but also exceed, the competition.

Krispy Kreme began as a small bakery that produced superior tasting donuts. They scoped out their major competition (Dunkin'

SECTION 2: Evaluating Your Options

Donuts) and determined that they had a better taste, one that the market would buy. They expanded quickly and the rest is history!

Being realistic about the quality of service you can offer is critical. **Our enthusiasm can lead us to overestimate what we can offer and underestimate what others can do.**

To illustrate, a small truck delivery service advertised that it could deliver cargo within two hours of its arrival in the city. But deliveries quickly fell behind schedule because the service owned only one truck. The promise was not upheld and they began to lose customers. A realistic review would have revealed the logistics of their system simply could not work. Other delivery services with multiple trucks were better equipped to serve this market.

• Longevity

Generally speaking, when a business has been around a long time, they are doing something right. Before taking the plunge, it would be to your advantage to understand the "secrets" that have kept them afloat long term. Then you can determine how and if you want to compete.

Some businesses tend to create more loyalty then others. A city that has two taxi companies that have both been in business a long time, with both offering comparable rates, and both providing good service, would make entering this business difficult.

Most customers have a tendency to stay with the familiar if it has been satisfactory. Even King Solomon wrote in Proverbs 27:10a,

"Do not forsake your own friend or your father's friend" (NASB). People have the habit of sticking with routine.

• Advertising and Image

When the competition already has a very strong image, then breaking into this particular market could require a lot of expensive advertising. For example, starting a magazine may require a $10 million dollar advertising investment just to get your project off the ground. Wisely and objectively determine what you will need to invest in advertising to reach and connect with potential customers.

In one town there are two companies who offer house inspections for home buyers. Both enjoy excellent reputations for service, thorough work, and customer satisfaction. A new player would have difficulty cracking into the market given the image and reputation of both companies. As King Solomon said, *"A good name is to be more desired than great riches"* (Proverbs 22:1, NASB).

In another city, eight companies offered home inspection service but none offered anything special. Ironically, getting realtors to give you a trial referral in this city of eight

How expensive is your advertising?

10

1

companies would be far easier than gaining referrals in the town with only two companies since both of the two offered exceptional service.

• Pricing

Determining how you can compete with current market pricing is important. Some customers will want to drive down your price, so you will have to determine in advance what your cost structure will look like, what you will be able to offer, and if that makes you competitive.

Your price must be based on what customers are willing to pay rather than based on your costs. Competing with companies (like Wal-Mart) who have the advantage of buying in massive quantities will probably not be possible. Their selling price may be lower than the actual wholesale cost of your product!

How competitive is your pricing?

Customers do not care about your product cost or the cost of running your business. Customers want the best value and successful businesses provide that value.

CONSIDER:

• Are you certain that you understand the competition?

• Is your niche a niche or are you competing with everyone else?

• Are you prepared for success?

ACTION STEPS:

1. Identify your niche in the marketplace.

2. Identify your competitors.

3. Identify the strengths and weaknesses of each.

4. Identify what actions you can take to compete successfully.

ROADMAP SIGNAL:

STOP: I am unable to determine actions that will surpass the competition's best efforts.

WAIT: I am unsure as to how I would stack up in the marketplace.

GO: I have a clear understanding of the competition, and what specific actions I can execute to succeed.

SECTION 2: Evaluating Your Options

CHAPTER 5

Defining Your Business Vision

A clear mission statement is fundamental to your business that you would have developed in chapter one. The mission statement helps you stay on track by establishing in advance the scope and target of your business. Hebrews 2:1 instructs, *"For this reason we must pay much closer attention to what we have heard, lest we drift away from it"* (NASB).

Further, by specifically articulating your mission statement, you will be able to clearly communicate your business focus to advisors, future customers and colleagues.

Your Mission Statement

Take the Chapter 1 mission statement that contains YOUR concise objectives and validate:
- **why your business exists**
- **what your main purpose will be**
- **what you do that others cannot do or cannot do as well**

Having such a statement will help you stay focused and on track by determining the size, scope, and goals of your business.

For example, the main purpose for the establishment of the Flagstaff Plant Nursery is to be a supplier of native plant material in the northern Arizona area. By staying with their mission statement, they do not become sidetracked into stocking plants imported from other locations. They stay focused on native plants and serving customers with that particular interest.

Next, decide on the objectives for your business. This will put the meat on the purpose you have established. The goal for the Flagstaff Plant Nursery, for instance, is not only to fulfill their purpose of supplying native plants, but also to become the leading native plant material supplier in northern Arizona. Becoming number one in this specific area of expertise is their objective.

Premier Log Homes of Flagstaff was established to build custom log homes ranging in size from 2,700 square feet to 6,000 square feet. Note their main purpose: building custom high-end log homes. They do not assemble homes from kits, remodel and repair, or build homes out of other materials.

When they receive inquiries and bid requests to assemble prefabricated homes or log home packages, they offer a quotation but do not spend a lot of time following up on those proposals. Most buyers of log home kits are looking for a lower-priced home, perhaps for a weekend getaway, rather than the highest level of quality and expertise.

Their mission statement also identified the Flagstaff area as their target. They determined that projects more than 60 miles away required too much travel time and expense, so those requests for bids are politely declined. By clearly determining their main purpose and objective, they are able to stay focused on their target or goal.

Some sample Mission Statements for builders might include:
- Catalina Homebuilding Company will develop well-planne housing communities in the southern Arizona area consisting of 300 homes per community with each home priced under $200,000.
- Thomas Custom Home Builders will provide comprehensive architectural and construction services on large acre plus lots throughout Arizona in the $600,000 to $1,200,000 cost range.

- Desert Home Development will plan, develop, and sell prefabricated homes in the Tucson region, ranging between $75,000 and $100,000 per home, with full amenities for those of retirement age.
- McKinney Construction will provide comprehensive design and construction services for the Tucson area, utilizing the best quality materials for updating kitchens and bathrooms.

In each example, the business owners had to determine what type of construction they would offer, make that their main purpose, and then expand on their objective.

While each of these firms shared the construction business as a general theme, you can see how their individual mission statements determined their specific goals and communicated to potential customers the area or focus of their business.

ASK YOURSELF:

- Do you know why your business exists?
- Do you know what your main purpose will be?
- What do you do that others cannot do or not do as well as you?
- What are your objectives for your business?
- Have you written out your mission statement?
- Have you identified your competitive advantage?

Your Business Vision Statement

Your business vision statement is a statement of how you desire your business to look in the future. It will determine the goals you set, that will, in turn, produce the results you desire as your business grows.

For example, painters do not merely decide what subject matter will be in their pictures. They must also decide the type of paint to be used (oil, acrylic, watercolor, etc), the time of day to be represented, the angle of the sun and accompanying shadows, and the general style of the picture (modern, classical, or impressionistic).

Just as a painter envisions the details of the final masterpiece before putting oil on the canvas, the business owner needs to develop a similar detailed goal-oriented process.

• What are your skills?

To begin, the owner must first consider the reality of the skills and competences they are able to bring to the process. To illustrate, Janet's, a small lunch counter owned by a great short-order cook, keeps the vision simple by serving breakfast and lunch items within 15 minutes of ordering. Janet's delivers this vision well, but if the owner were to turn her great lunch counter into a gourmet European restaurant, she would not have the skill or passion to accomplish that vision.

Likewise, if Desert Home Development wanted to change from selling prefabricated homes in a planned community to building million dollar custom homes, they would lack the skills and competency to compete in this market. **Keep your vision in line with what you can do well!**

Initially, your business may not be everything you envision. However, by deciding in advance what your vision will be and the kind of business you want to build, every step can be designed to move you toward your goal. Remember what the prophet Habakkuk wrote, *"For there is still a vision for the appointed time; it speaks of the end, and does not lie. If it seems to tarry, wait for it; it will surely come, it will not delay"* (Habakkuk 2:3, NRSV).

SECTION 3: Defining Your Business

- ## Clarify your vision

To achieve the best results, you will need to develop a vision for three key aspects of your business:

#1 VISION FOR PRODUCTS & SERVICE

Developing a vision for your products and service will help both you and your team to understand exactly what products or service you will deliver, how the delivery will be accomplished, and the general impression you wish to present. The Lord instructed Moses, *"See that you make them after the pattern for them, which was shown to you on the mountain"* (Exodus 25:40, NASB). God had a pattern, gave that vision to Moses, and Moses transferred that vision to the people, enabling them to follow through.

The vision for McKinney Construction is providing creative design services for kitchens and baths using high quality finished products. The vision includes having nice company shirts with the McKinney logo emblazed on the front. McKinney wants to create an impression that meets the expectations of high-end customers.

In contrast, a firm specializing in kitchen remodeling that caters to the budget-minded customer may establish a vision that includes economical delivery and staff that wear average, non-descript clothing.

A vision for customer service for a fast food restaurant may be to take every order within four minutes of arrival and to serve the food to customers within five minutes of ordering. To consistently execute that time vision, the restaurant must be organized in every arena, including the equipment selected, the menu items chosen, and the proper training of the staff. Any bottlenecks that occur which thwart the vision must be addressed.

Catalina Home Building, having a mission to provide quality homes priced under $200,000, will need its vision to include efficient home design and land utilization, the placement of five homes on every

SECTION 3: Defining Your Business

acre, and limiting customer choice to four model plans in order to keep down costs. Other parts of their vision may include: on time delivery, defect-free homes, and upholding a policy of honesty with customers, employees, and suppliers.

Determining and clarifying your product or service vision not only allows you to keep yourself and your staff focused, but it also helps you target the right customer with your marketing and advertising dollars. The method used to reach the buyer of $800,000 custom homes is very different than targeting a buyer for homes under $200,000.

When you are clear about your vision, you can clearly communicate with your perspective customers. A key factor in building repeat business is to make sure your customers know what they can expect, and then faithfully fulfill that expectation every time.

#2 VISION FOR YOUR WORK AND STAFF

Next, develop a vision for your staff regarding how you expect them to execute responsibilities and service customers. It is important to develop your employee vision before the first team member is even hired.

Jill, owner of Clear Expectations Window Cleaning, has a vision to present cleanliness in every aspect of her service delivery. She charges a bit more, but strives to impress the customer at every turn. Each team member of the window cleaning company is expected to wear an assigned uniform, and when working inside, a cloth "sock" is to be worn over their shoes to ensure the customer's carpets are not soiled.

When hiring team members, Jill evaluates appearance and manners and explains clearly what is expected of them. Jill instructs employees how to introduce themselves and how to politely interact with customers. She instructs them to return any furniture to the original spot after cleaning.

Jill is looking for people who have the same heart for excellence as she does. Scripture states, *"The Lord has sought out for Himself a man after His own heart"* (1 Samuel 13:14b, NASB). Likewise, you need to build a work team with people who will faithfully execute **your** vision.

An antique furniture restoration firm in Ohio specializes in high quality antique furniture restoration. They are quite expensive but they provide outstanding results. One of the visions for their staff is practicing patience while executing attention to detail. They do not hire the fastest workers, but instead strive to hire those who fulfill their vision of attention to detail.

Steve, the owner of the restoration firm, has seen many good furniture restorers lack the perseverance to work out every defect and smooth every surface prior to applying the final finish to the furniture. In his business, Steve teaches new workers what products to apply to each type of wood and which sanding products he wants used to obtain the desired results. Steve is able to share his vision of quality work every day with his employees, resulting in a magnificent final product.

Steve then markets his vision to potential customers. He proudly invites prospective customers to come into his shop and see how the utmost care is poured into every piece of furniture. Customers then have the confidence to turn over their prized 18th century heirlooms for restoration.

Southwest Airlines has a vision for their planes to land and take off from each airport in a timely manner. The CEO understands that the airline does not make any money when the plane is sitting at the gate. Every staff member, including flight crew, cabin attendants, and gate agents understand that goal.

As a result, Southwest Airlines hires people that demonstrate a reasonable sense of urgency in completing tasks. When crewmembers are trained, each person is taught what steps need to be taken to execute the company's vision. Every team member knows the directive: get planes landing and taking off both safely and fast. When God spoke to Ezekiel, He said, *"Son of man, look with your eyes and hear with your ears and pay attention to everything I am going to show you, for that is why you have been brought here"* (Ezekiel 40:4, NIV). As the Lord was careful in instructing Ezekiel, you need to be careful when instructing your staff.

#3 VISION FOR COMPANY ORGANIZATION

Lastly, you will need to develop a vision for how you want your business to operate. For example, Catalina Home Building Company provides furnished models for prospective customers to see in order to choose a plan for their own home. Brochures are available that cover the basic cost of each plan along with a list of pricing for additional home options. Prospects are encouraged to browse with little customer interaction until a strong buying interest is expressed.

The company believes the product is impressive enough to sell itself. Rather than invest thousands of dollars for a large staff of sales people, they put that savings back into the homes they build.

On the other hand, Thomas Custom Home Builders spends a great deal of time with prospective purchasers and has a vision that includes their staff understanding basic architectural principles, building materials, and building requirements for difficult locations. A fast food restaurant in a local town has established a vision that includes quick service and low cost. Speed and efficiency are built into every step. Both their environment and their staff exemplify the fast-paced vision.

In the same town are two expensive restaurants that have a comparable menu and pricing, but each has a very different vision of how they will operate. One has a high-energy environment with trendy colors, fast-paced music, and a staff that moves quickly from table to table. Across the street, the other restaurant features a quiet atmosphere with a more traditional décor and a staff who functions at a more leisurely pace. Each place does well, but the visions of how each place functions are very different.

The vision for Wal-Mart stores is to offer low prices. They achieve the lowest possible prices from suppliers and maintain the most efficient low cost operation possible. An additional key element of Wal-Mart's vision is to use technology as a tool for keeping costs down and their stores efficient. To satisfy that vision, inventory is maintained in real time at every store. Should a customer purchase 12 bottles of a particular shampoo, reducing the inventory to two bottles by 9:30 a.m., an order is immediately generated and replacement inventory is shipped that same day. Wal-Mart's vision to keep shelves stocked while keeping inventory to a minimum is possible through the use of current available technology.

A trucking company also has a vision to use technology as a competitive advantage. As a result, a large investment has been made to purchase a system that directly interfaces with customers. These customers can have direct access to the trucking system and place orders themselves for pick- up. Every part of the process is automated so the customer can trace online, in real time, each shipment. While this system is more expensive to install and operate, some customers find that having up-to-the-minute information is worth their cost.

Another motor carrier has a vision of being the lowest cost trucker, and to execute that vision, costs are kept down at every opportunity. The technology selected by that carrier is designed to improve operating efficiency for the trucker, not enhance service to the customer. As a result, the low budget trucker offers rates about 15% less then the other firm. The bottom line is that both businesses are successful.

SECTION 3: Defining Your Business

CONSIDER:

- Both your mission statement and business vision statement need to be in harmony with God's teaching.

- We are instructed in I Corinthians to do whatever we do to the glory of God.

- Step back and prayerfully ask yourself, "Is every part of my vision honoring to God?"

- Ask yourself, "Is everything I have planned pleasing to the Lord?"

- If so, move forward, but if not, then rethink your vision and make adjustments.

- You will want to position yourself in the best possible way for God's favor, aid, wisdom, and blessing as you embark on your new venture.

ACTION STEPS:

1. Write out your business vision for your product or service.

2. Write out a vision for your work and staff.

3. Write out your vision for the organization.

4. Can you see yourself executing this vision?

ROADMAP SIGNAL:

STOP: I am confused.

WAIT: I am unclear as to my mission and vision.

GO: I have a clear mission and vision for my business.

CHAPTER 6

Making Your Business Choice

There are three ways to start a business:
1. **buy an ongoing business**
2. **purchase a franchise**
3. **start your own enterprise from scratch**

Each has advantages and disadvantages. The key is to review each possibility carefully before making your decision.

Option #1: Buy An Ongoing Business

An ongoing business provides several strong advantages: a customer base, an established reputation, an operating system already in place, and a track record of generating profit and cash flow (hopefully).

Generally, purchasing an ongoing operation is less risky. The first concerns have already been addressed: that the business model works and that customers have been established.

If you do choose to buy an ongoing business, then be sure that you:

• Find the right business

Use the resources available that can assist you in finding a business to purchase. Most cities have one or more business brokers who list businesses for sale. These brokers charge a commission, usually between 5% and 15%, to the seller or buyer, or both. Newspaper advertisements and real estate brokers also carry business listings.

- **Stay focused**

Consider only businesses that fulfill the mission you want and use the skills you have previously determined. Do not be tempted to drift off mission just because a business looks like a good deal or you believe it will generate cash beyond your wildest dreams. This is not the proper motivation for choosing a business. Only by sticking to your mission will you succeed long term.

- **Evaluate the ongoing business**

If you find a business that peaks your interest, then you are ready to begin the process of taking a closer look. Three general business areas are important to carefully review:
1. **what is on paper**
2. **the business operation itself**
3. **the customer base.**

#1 INSPECT WHAT IS ON PAPER:

Every business has or should have an income statement, cash flow statement, balance sheet, tax return, and inventory list. Each of these documents tells a story and placed together you will get a clear idea of how the business is doing.

Be advised that financial statements are only a picture of the past but not a guarantee of the future.

INCOME STATEMENT

The **income statement** will give you an indication of the money that has been made, if any, by the business. This statement should be discussed line by line with the seller.

One business owner showed a net profit on his income statement of $50,000 from the previous year. Upon closer review it was noted that neither the owner nor his partner had taken a salary. If a market salary had been added to the expenses, the business would have lost $45,000 rather than made $50,000—a major difference!"

At other times, expenses that are more personal in nature can be buried under the general heading of business expenses. Again, to prevent any confusion, insist on an explanation of every item in detail. If the seller starts making everything terribly complex, that is a sign they may be "blowing smoke" to cover something.

CASH FLOW

Cash flow will confirm, or not, that the business is indeed making money. Otherwise you will find yourself struggling.

Look for any differences between the income statement and the cash flow statement. For example, an income statement may show $100,000 profit while cash flow is zero. If accounts receivable have increased by $100,000, then you need to know that those larger receivables are collectable. Whenever you see a difference between income and cash flow, make sure you understand the basis for that difference and are comfortable with the reason.

BALANCE SHEET

The **balance sheet** should give you a sense of the "net worth" of the business. In theory, the net worth on the balance sheet should be a reflection of what the company's assets would sell for on the open market.

Unfortunately, the balance sheet can be misleading. Some equipment may be fully depreciated and worth more than is stated on the balance sheet, while other equipment may be overstated. A computer purchased three months ago for $2,500 may be listed as a $2,200 asset but have a market value of only $400.

Inventory claims also need to be challenged. I reviewed a custom window supply business and questioned the $125,000 value placed on the current inventory. I knew that all the work they did was custom ordered. In reality, while the inventory was listed at cost, the inventory was comprised of "mistakes" in custom orders that could not be delivered; these mistakes were stored and listed as inventory. In reality, the $125,000 in inventory was worth about $15,000.

Check carefully concerning how old or stale the merchandise is and compare that to the usual turnaround time for that inventory. If most goods are normally sold within a 60-day period, be suspicious of the actual value of any goods still stocked after 120 days.

An art gallery carried a full line of artwork and accessories made by a well-known artist. Some of the product line sold well, while other products failed to sell. Of the carried inventory listed at $150,000, over $100,000 of that amount had been in stock for more than a year. In such cases, it would be wise to either offer to buy the stale inventory at a steep discount or refuse to take it at all.

INTANGIBLE ASSETS

Intangible assets are often listed as business assets. An intangible asset, like community goodwill, is hard to define and not marketable.

An insurance agency was carrying over $75,000 of goodwill based on a recent buy out of a partner. You would not want to pay for intangible assets that do not directly represent value to you.

INCOME TAX STATEMENTS

Income tax statements for the business or owners (if separate tax returns were not filed) should be made available. The tax return should agree with the income statement. A tax return sent to the IRS is less commonly fudged than a non-audited financial statement.

Beware of any explanations that indicate the business really made more money than is represented on the tax return. For instance, I was asked to review documents for a couple interested in purchasing an independent dairy bar. The seller told them, "While I showed a $55,000 profit on my tax return, I really make over $150,000 each year. I just take some of the cash home." The seller was either lying to the couple or to the IRS. I asked the couple if they really wanted to do business with someone they knew for certain was a liar.

Lack of honesty or integrity in any part of the financial information is reason to stop all forward movement regardless of how good everything looks.

#2 INSPECT THE OVERALL BUSINESS OPERATION:

Get an overall picture of how the business is being run. Doing some simple observations and checking around on your own can prevent costly errors or an unwise purchase.

MAINTENANCE AND REPAIRS

Maintenance and repairs left undone can accumulate quickly and add surplus costs. Take a good look around. Dirty bathrooms are quick indicators that other maintenance has been neglected. Items that can be easily cleaned up or fixed with a coat of paint are no big deal, so look deeper.

I walked through one business for sale and noticed the parking lot was in need of immediate resurfacing. In addition, the roof leaked.

These were two expensive repairs that had been neglected. Make sure any offer you give for a business takes into account the expense of maintenance and repairs.

LEGAL ISSUES

Legal issues can be incredible costly. Check to see if there are any outstanding legal problems as well as any complaints that have been filed with the Better Business Bureau. If the business requires licensing, look into any complaints filed with the regulating authorities.

INTERNAL IMPROVEMENTS

Internal improvements are always possible. Ask yourself, "How can I add value to this business? How can I make this business better? If you observe problems, make sure that they are the kind of problems that you can correct.

I reviewed a medical practice that was for sale and found the billing system was a mess. The insurance billing was handled so poorly that thousands of dollars had to be written off each month as a result. The doctor who was considering the purchase of this practice knew that his current system could easily correct the problem, increase cash flow, and improve profits.

#3 INSPECT THE CUSTOMER BASE:

Customers are the mother's milk of any business and you should make every effort to access the status of existing relationships. Talk with customers if you are looking at a retail or restaurant business. Spend several days just observing customers to determine if they look satisfied. If possible, ask customers what they like most and least about the business.

• Negotiating your purchase

After you have decided to move forward, negotiating the purchase price is the next step. Unfortunately, there are no set formulas that cover every business. Care must be exercised to offer only a price that will work for you. Buying a business that fails to cover your salary, for example, will not work.

Your accountant can give you some guidelines, but generally, the more the business has been dependent directly on the original owner for success, the lower the price you may want to offer. An accounting practice or a high quality restaurant may have been very dependent on the skill and dedication of the owner, while a corner grocery store may have been more dependent on its location and selection of merchandise.

If you ask the seller to carry back financing, you will still need to put down between 30-50% of the purchase price. Cash buyers can often negotiate a better price.

Option #2: Buy A Franchise

A franchise can provide many benefits to business owners. When you buy a franchise you profit from the experience of others and receive a business model that has demonstrated results. You and your staff will be trained on how to be successful in your new venture. In some turnkey operations, a location site has been pre-selected to ensure a good return on your investment.

• Does the "shoe fit"?

If you want to investigate franchise opportunities, make sure the business is a fit for both your passion and skills. Visit and speak to others who have operated the same type of franchise you may be interested in purchasing. Do not just call the list of references furnished by the franchising company, but call others as well.

SECTION 3: Defining Your Business

In one case, I called the stores given as references by the franchiser and received overall positive recommendations. However, when I called others not listed, I received a very different story. You will want to find out if the start-up claims made by the franchising company were true, how responsive the company has been to concerns, what unanticipated problems were encountered, and if the income projections were accurate.

When operating a franchise, you also need to be a person who enjoys doing things in a consistent manner. When you walk into a McDonald's restaurant you will notice every burger, fry, and salad will be made the same, according to the established pattern. You need to determine if following a specific blueprint for business suits your personality.

• Where to look

Trade shows are held nationally where you can investigate a wide variety of possibilities. Spending a few hundred or a few thousand dollars in travel expenses may pay huge dividends later. Just be careful not to sign agreements at the show. Allow time to do your review and avoid making a decision too quickly that you may regret.

• The purchase price

When purchasing a franchise, an up front fee is generally paid to the franchiser and then an ongoing percent of the receipts is paid long term. Most often, you get what you pay for. Many "low cost" operators lack a good long-term track record, while a more-established franchise (like a McDonalds) may cost well over one million dollars but will have an excellent track record.

When reviewing business possibilities, take into consideration the total cash outlay needed. For example, the up front fee may be low, but you may be required to purchase a large amount of merchandise or inventory, raising the cost significantly.

Also, check to see how much of the ongoing royalty payments are re-invested into the business for things like advertising, developing new products, and continued training of staff, rather than being absorbed as overhead or profits for the franchiser.

Option #3: Start From Scratch

Starting from scratch may require a lower initial investment, but it holds the highest risk of failure since you do not have a proven model to follow. When starting from zero, you need to develop the complete vision, the entire business system, and the marketing plan.

If you have a true desire to start your own business from scratch, you will need to carefully follow the steps discussed throughout this book.

CONSIDER:

• Take some time to absorb the information in this chapter over the next few days.

• Perhaps you have had your initial instincts confirmed for the type of business approach that would work for you.

• Or, perhaps you have new things to consider that had not been clear before now.

• Beginning a new business is an exciting and sometimes intimidating process.

• By taking the time to thoroughly consider all your options and being assured your final choice is a perfect fit for your skills and passion, you will have created a plan for your greatest enjoyment and success.

ACTION STEPS:

1. Would my personality fit buying a franchise?

2. Do I have the money and experience to purchase an ongoing business?

3. If yes, have I identified possibilities?

4. Create a list of key questions to ask and be answered.

5. Do I want to start a business from scratch?

ROADMAP SIGNAL:

STOP: I cannot find a business opportunity I can afford or that suits my temperament.

WAIT: I have not answered every question.

GO: I have completed my homework and understand what business opportunity I can afford and will suit me personally.

CHAPTER 7

Choosing Your Business Format

Before you can begin your business, you will have to select the business format that reflects your needs and circumstances. Then you must become acquainted with the logistics and procedures for the format you have chosen.

Businesses are organized in one of three formats:

- Sole proprietorships
- Partnerships
- Corporations.

Format #1: Sole proprietorships

A sole proprietorship business structure is the simplest and least costly to implement. It works well when the business is not too complex and is owned by either one person or a married couple.

• Separate business and personal expenses

In a sole proprietorship both business expenses and income are taxed and paid by you personally. If you have a start-up loss, you can deduct the loss on your tax return. You will need to separate your business expenses from personal expenses. I suggest keeping a separate checking account and a separate credit/debit card that is used for business expenses only. Otherwise your business expenses will become hopelessly entangled with your personal expenses.

Another reason to keep things separate is to clarify whether you are making money or not. Bill was working as a sole proprietor doing home remodeling. When he purchased office supplies and work tools in addition to buying gas for his truck, Bill charged them all on the family credit card. According to his records he was making a "profit" of $50,000 on the business, but when his expenses were deducted, the "profit" was reduced to $30,000 — a substantial difference!

As a sole proprietor, you are personally responsible for any liabilities and therefore will need to carry adequate liability coverage. Also, since any profits will be taxed to you personally, you need to make quarterly income and self-employment tax payments to the government. Should you elect to borrow money, your ability to borrow will rely solely on your personal credit history. (However, borrowing is not encouraged in Scripture.)

Format #2: Business Partnerships

Partnerships are one of the most common forms of business organization **and unfortunately also the least successful**. Fewer than five percent of all business partnerships survive intact long term.

> **Fewer than five percent of all business partnerships survive intact long term.**

If you are in a business partnership or thinking about forming one, you should consider carefully the reality of these odds. But if you follow biblical principles in establishing and maintaining your partnership, you can improve your prospects for success and minimize possible painful experiences.

• A firm foundation

Christians should only form partnerships with other Christian believers. As the apostle Paul wrote, *"Do not be mismatched with unbelievers. For what partnership is there between righteousness and lawlessness? Or what fellowship is there between light and darkness?"* (2 Corinthians 6:14, NRSV).

Paul knew that if two oxen of unequal strength were yoked together, the pair would travel in a circle, getting nowhere. Similarly, business decisions will be difficult if partners have unequal value systems.

Effective partnerships are built on a firm foundation of understanding. The number one reason for conflict in a business partnership is lack of agreement on key issues. In a partnership, it is important to first establish a sound scriptural basis for how decisions will be made. God asks us through the prophet Amos, *"Do two walk together unless they have agreed to do so?"* (Amos 3:3, NIV). Agreeing on how you will resolve key business issues will provide a firm foundation for future success.

Unresolved disagreement creates tension that will hamper, if not mortally wound, the partnership. *"Through presumption comes nothing but strife"* wrote King Solomon (Proverbs 13:10, NASB). The time to discuss tough issues is before the business is started. Then put your agreements in writing because time has a way of confusing and distorting our memories.

• Eleven issues for agreement

The following are 11 key issues where agreement is essential before you launch a partnership. Take your time to examine each one. Rushing ahead without proper evaluation can spell your demise. *"The plans of the diligent lead surely to advantage, But everyone who is hasty comes surely to poverty"* (Proverbs 21:5, NASB).

KEY #1: ESTABLISH YOUR MISSION

You must first agree on your purpose for entering business. Two builders who started a contracting business later found out that one partner wanted to focus on remodeling while the other wanted to build new homes. A thorough discussion and agreement in advance would have avoided such arguments. Both partners had a worthy vision; they were just different. Lack of a common vision between partners will cause any business to falter.

KEY #2: AGREE THAT YOU WILL SUBMIT TO BIBLICAL AUTHORITY FOR RUNNING YOUR BUSINESS

The Lord gave Joshua wise advice when He said, *"This book of the law shall not depart from your mouth, but you shall meditate on it day and night, so that you may be careful to do according to all that is written in it; for then you will make your way prosperous, and then you will have success"* (Joshua 1:8, NASB).

Obedience to Scripture will bring blessings. Agreeing with your partner to use biblical authority as the basis for decisions, policies, and business management will provide a firm foundation for your operation.

KEY #3: DETERMINE IN ADVANCE WHO WILL BE THE MANAGING PARTNER

Jesus taught, *"No one can serve two masters"* (Matthew 6:24, NKJV). A business cannot ultimately have two bosses. Of course, the partner or partners who agree to submit to a managing partner must have confidence that their partner has the skill, ability, and temperament to lead effectively, without disregarding the input and feelings of the other partner(s).

KEY #4: EVALUATE THE LONG AND SHORT-TERM EXPECTATIONS OF EACH PARTNER

How big you want the business to be, how much time each partner will invest, and other key goals and standards need to be defined and agreed on in advance. Your ideas may change over time, but failure to agree up front is guaranteed to cause major disharmony.

A young attorney who formed a legal partnership with two of his friends wanted to build the practice into a national firm that would employ scores of attorneys. His partners, however, wanted simply to generate enough revenue to earn a living. Both expectations were reasonable, but they were incompatible. As a result, none of the partners were happy.

KEY #5: CLEARLY DEFINE HOW MUCH MONEY EACH PARTNER WILL INVEST AND WHAT YOU WILL DO IF MORE MONEY IS NEEDED LATER

Financial investment is a common point of conflict. Unfortunately, it is all too common for businesses to require additional infusions of cash, and if the partners are unable or unwilling to invest, the business may collapse or need to be sold. If the financial investment between partners is unequal, determine in advance and put it in writing how that will affect decision-making control and future investment.

Sometimes a partner will invest his or her expertise in lieu of money. For example, two partners might find a restaurant where one partner invests $300,000 in equipment, advertising, and start-up expenses, while the other partner, an expert chef, manages the establishment. As long as both partners agree on the value of the chef's "sweat equity," this kind of arrangement can work. However, problems can arise if the business needs more cash and the partners cannot agree on how to proceed.

KEY #6: WRITE A BUSINESS PLAN

Jesus said, *"For which of you, intending to build a tower, does not first sit down and estimate the cost, to see whether he has enough to complete it?"* (Luke 14:28, NRSV). Writing a business plan is a challenging but necessary exercise if you want your partnership to succeed. Effective business planning will keep the entire team focused on your key goals and objectives.

KEY #7: DECIDE HOW PROFITS WILL BE DISTRIBUTED

Reinvesting some profits in the business will be necessary to grow the enterprise. Problems may surface when the distribution of profits has not been determined in advance. One partner may want to invest all the profits to grow the business while others may want to receive additional income. Normally, initial profits are reinvested and some future profits may be distributed. The key is agreement in advance.

KEY #8: DETERMINE THE DIVISION OF WORK RESPONSIBILITIES

The apostle Paul wrote, *"For as we have many members in one body, but all the members do not have the same function"* (Romans 12:4, NKJV). A good inventory of spiritual gifts along with a personality profile can be of great assistance in determining responsibilities between partners. Identify which skills and competencies are needed and then fill out the partnership team to create the proper balance.

I observed one example of efficient division of leadership at an auto parts firm established by three partners. One partner is an effective administrator and he became the managing partner for finance and administration. Another was responsible for production and quality control. The third partner was in charge of marketing and sales. By matching each person with his most effective role, the partners were able to operate a successful business.

Any business start-up will require a major commitment of time. Different priorities between partners may spell trouble. The key is to establish regular work hours for each partner, keeping the proper sequence of priority: Lord, family, and then work.

KEY #9: ESTABLISH COMPANY POLICIES

A policy is a statement of what a business will always do or never do. These policies become a foundation for every business decision. For example, what is your customer-return policy? Employment practices? Pricing structure? Management controls? Written policies will help the business stay on track and maintain consistency. Policies should address every major issue and skip the immaterial issues.

KEY #10: COMPILE A SET OF BUSINESS PROCEDURES THAT COVER EVERY ASPECT OF THE BUSINESS

Whether your business is large or small, written procedures are essential for establishing effective operations. The book of Judges relates, *"In those days Israel had no king; everyone did as he saw fit"* (Judges 21:25, NIV).

The absence of clear procedures will create a business environment with inconsistent standards resulting in more errors, higher costs, and erratic customer service. Policies and procedures will allow new employees to be more effective and provide a road map to determine when partners need to help out due to workload issues or vacations. When the procedures are developed, copies should be placed in a binder and given to each partner and member. Better to start with simple procedures and refine as you go rather than to be caught with "analysis paralysis" and never get started.

KEY #11: DECIDE IN ADVANCE HOW AND UNDER WHAT CIRCUMSTANCES A PARTNERSHIP WILL BE DISSOLVED

In the excitement of starting a new enterprise, no one wants to discuss the possibility of dissolving the partnership — but that is precisely when the conversation must take place. After all, most partnerships will terminate at some point and failure to have a buy/sell agreement in place will create a monstrous headache. Do not put off this important discussion until later thinking that you will work everything out in a fair way when the time comes.

• Seek wise counsel

Before you establish a partnership, obtain and listen to wise counsel. *"Where there is no counsel, the people fall; but in the multitude of counselors there is safety"* (Proverbs 11:14, NKJV).

Seek counsel from three perspectives: legal, financial, and business. Each partner should find a friend or business advisor — someone who knows them well — and ask them to review the business plan and work commitment and gain their perspective about what has been set up. This advisor should also give feedback about how the opportunity fits with the individuals embarking on the business. Even a good business plan will not suit certain personalities.

Also, if you are married, always seek counsel from your spouse. Never enter into a partnership unless your spouse is in complete agreement and understands all the commitments and liabilities of the venture. If you do not take time to agree before the business begins, you will pay a much greater price later.

• Communicate!

Once you have decided to move forward with your business and the proper steps have been taken to establish a business plan, your next challenge is to establish an ongoing and effective communication system. As your enterprise moves forward, hitches will inevitably develop. Communication is imperative within the partnership to effectively work through these snags.

Establish regular meeting times and keep the lines of communication open. During the start-up period, daily briefings and reviews may be necessary. Once the business is established, you may get by with meeting less frequently, but make sure not to lose touch with each other. Partners should come prepared to discuss any significant production, customer service, financial, or personal issue. When items are brought to the table, identify which are for communication, decision-making, or information only.

• Conflict resolution

Conflict resolution should follow the biblical standard outlined in Matthew that states, *"If your brother sins, go and reprove him in private"* (18:15a, NASB). Next, if the issue is not resolved, *"Take one or two more with you, so that BY THE MOUTH OF TWO OR THREE WITNESSES EVERY FACT MAY BE CONFIRMED"* (18:16, NASB, emphasis added). This may involve bringing up the issue with all the partners.

Often, in our humanness, we will be inclined to discuss our complaints with others instead of confronting the issue squarely with the person with whom we have a concern. Ultimately, this causes dissension and a loss of morale within the business.

A partner who has made a commitment prior to starting the business may later want to change it. However, *"It is better not to vow than to make a vow and not fulfill it"* (Ecclesiastes. 5:5, NIV). All vows, including agreements made upon entering a partnership, need to be honored. So be careful and think through every commitment from a long-term perspective before you give your word.

Workloads including over-time requirements may shift or be different from what was expected. Inevitably, adjustments will be needed. The apostle Paul wrote, *"Carry each other's burdens, and in this way you will fulfill the law of Christ"* (Galatians 6:2, NIV). A spirit of teamwork within the partnership will be necessary for success. Evaluate the workflow on a regular basis and adjust as necessary.

• Effective goals

Every partner must establish personal work goals that fit into the entire business plan. Effective goals will be specific, measurable, accomplishment-focused, realistic, and timed or tied to the business.

Most of us do not like to be held accountable, but as Paul instructed Timothy, *"Take pains with these things; be absorbed in them, so your progress may be evident to all"* (1 Timothy 4:15, NASB). Effective partnerships are transparent partnerships, where each partner agrees to be held accountable to achieve success. Our partnerships should reflect the model given in Ephesians 5:21 of a marriage partnership: *"Submit to one another out of reverence for Christ"* (NRSV).

• Finances

No one partner or individual should have unlimited control over the finances. This is often a recipe for disaster. A corporation of four partners suffered a loss of $300,000 (two years worth of profit) when the partner entrusted with the financial responsibility embezzled the funds.

Even the 12 disciples suffered financial loss. John relates that Judas *"was a thief, and as he had the money box, he used to pilfer what was put into it"* (John 12:6b, NASB). Always require two signatures on all large checks and regularly conduct an independent bookkeeping review.

• Forgiveness

When our partners fall short of the mark, we need to foster a sprit of confession and forgiveness using the biblical model. First, we are called to *"confess* [our sins or shortcomings] *to each other"* (James 5:16a, NIV), and readily admit our mistakes. When we mess up, we need to offer an apology. Additionally, true repentance not only requires a confession, but a change of future actions. As Jesus told the woman caught in adultery, *"From now on sin no more"* (John 8:11b, NASB).

• Dissolving a partnership

For whatever the reason, a partnership might need to be dissolved. Perhaps one partner failed to meet the commitments made before the partnership was established or perhaps one partner moved to another city to pursue a new venture.

Regardless of the reason for the separation, if the time comes to part ways, the Bible offers an excellent model. *"Abram said to Lot, 'Please let there be no strife between you and me, nor between my herdsmen and your herdsmen, for we are brothers. Is not the whole land before you? Please separate from me: if to the left, then I will go to the right; or if to the right, then I will go to the left'"* (Genesis 13:8-9, NASB).

When partners cannot agree on a resolution, following this model allows one partner to propose a solution that can then be ratified by the other partner or partners. If the proposal is balanced, then either option will be fair.

I always recommend that Christians agree in advance to have any disputes resolved through mediation or binding arbitration in accordance with the Institute for Christian Conciliation's Rules of Procedure or specify the use of Peacemakers ministries. This allows disputes to be resolved promptly, at reasonable cost, and without utilizing the public legal system.

SECTION 3: Defining Your Business

Format #3: Corporations

If you choose the third option, that of forming a corporation with one or more people, then I suggest using the same principles of evaluation and agreement that you have just read in regard to forming a partnership.

Consider the following advantages and disadvantages of using the corporate format:

ADVANTAGE: You receive some protection in liability

Unless you have signed personally for obligations or have given your personal guarantee, you generally are not personally responsible for any debts of the corporation. When you are just starting out, however, many vendors or landlords will require a personal guarantee; once you give that guarantee you will be personally responsible for payment, corporation or not.

ADVANTAGE: You can sell shares to investors

Obtain legal advice to ensure you comply with all required securities laws in your state, regardless of how little money is invested.

ADVANTAGE: Retained earnings are not taxed

If you decide to keep some of the profits in the business, corporate tax may need to be paid, but any retained earnings are not taxed personally. If two or more people form a corporation, rather than establishing a partnership, the decisions can be made according to the amount of stock held. Three "partners" holding 60% of the shares can exert their will over two shareholders owning 40% of the stock.

DISADVANTAGE: Attorney fees are required to handle the paperwork

All corporate entities established must conform to all federal and state laws. An attorney can help ensure you comply with the fine print.

DISADVANTAGE: You have to incorporate under the laws of your state and then comply with all the laws of your state

Incorporating in a different state where you live may add complications. For example, a group advertises the "advantages" of incorporating in Nevada. Most states require that income be declared and taxes paid in the state where that income was earned. Setting up a corporation in another state just to dodge local taxes is generally illegal.

DISADVANTAGE: Profits taken by the owner would require taxes to be paid by the corporation first and then again by the individual

Note: An S Corporation is an option for owners who want to set up a corporation but have all the income and loss flow to them personally, avoiding the problem of double taxation.

DISADVANTAGE: Corporations require more structure than partnerships or proprietorships

These structures include electing a director and officers as well as keeping minute books.

Reminder: If you are forming a corporation with other people, you should follow the guidelines in the partnership section to avoid future problems.

SECTION 3: Defining Your Business

CONSIDER:

• Whether you choose a sole proprietorship, a business partnership, or a corporate format, you will need to pay close attention to the requirements, advantages, and disadvantages of each approach.

• In addition, be sure to include the personalities of those involved in your choice.

• Not every business format, however fine, works for every person.

• Many times your choice of format will be obvious but sometimes it is not that clear.

• Take the time to re-read this chapter slowly and prayerfully to see where you are being led.

• God expects us to use good common sense and to avail ourselves of proper information as part of our decision-making process.

• You have to be an active participant in discerning what is best for your future.

ACTION STEPS:

1. Determine the business format that is right for you.

2. Do I need to attract investors, and if so, am I willing to surrender some control?

3. Determine what format is best to execute the business mission and vision, not necessarily what you personally prefer.

ROADMAP SIGNAL:

STOP: I have no idea what type of organization would work best.

WAIT: I think I know, but am not sure I can answer why one type of organization is best.

GO: I am clear, and can state why, a type of business organization would best suit my needs, and the vision for the business.

SECTION 3: Defining Your Business

CHAPTER 8

Preparing Your Business Plan

Tom had been a crackerjack real estate salesman and then a successful real estate broker, combining 20 years of experience between the two. He knew the business well and had a knack for negotiating prices and closing deals. Tom felt the time was right to strike out on his own. He resigned from his job, rented office space down the street, put out a sign, and was in business for himself.

Tom was tired of being the star salesman and having to give up a large part of his commission to the company he worked for. By being in business for himself, he would be able to keep 100% of the money!

Tom started with two employees—a receptionist and an office clerk to keep up with the paperwork. He believed that with his extensive contacts, his business would be generating cash within three months. However, after four months, business was slow and most of his start-up cash was depleted. More cash was going out than coming in.

It was time to tighten things up. Tom let the receptionist go, and shortly afterwards, released the office clerk. Phone calls were taken by an answering machine and often a dozen messages would jam his cell phone. Because Tom was now on his own, no one was able to back him up. His old contacts, when they did call, never received the service they had in the past. Tom was wearing too many hats.

Tom felt the only answer was to work harder, showing properties by day and doing computer searches and market research by night. Soon he was working 16-18 hours a day, seven days a week, with very little result. The more hours he worked, the smaller the return. Ultimately, after 18 months, he closed his business $60,000 poorer and with his marriage strained.

A Review Of Tom's "Plan"

Of course, none of use would make the same mistakes Tom did, but let's review them nonetheless:

• No plan

Tom never compiled a written and researched business plan. His "plan" was basically in his head and was based solely on his experience as a salesman and broker. Tom felt he already "knew" what to do, but he failed to collect information and data that would help him fulfill his dream in a concrete and well-executed manner.

• Lack of knowledge

The fact that a new real estate office generates little business its first month was something Tom did not know. Had he known that, he wouldn't have hired staff immediately, which drained $6,000 of precious operating cash. He could have focused his first 30 days on marketing to his extensive list of contacts, telling them he was now on his own. Additionally, there were several neighborhoods where he was considered a leading expert. Sending a mailing to those areas would have reinforced his market presence.

• No planning

With careful planning, Tom's receptionist (hired during the second month) could have been given other duties besides answering the phone. Then Tom could have been more responsive to clients, while still saving the salary for the second office person. By not making the second hire he would have been able to carry the receptionist another four months.

• No target market

Though Tom had an extensive contact list, the past clients would probably only generate business down the line, maybe years down the line. Tom needed an income stream immediately. He should have selected a target market and pursued that market.

• Too much with too little

Tom also expected to be profitable within six months, figuring $30,000 would cover his opening costs plus the initial loses. Unfortunately, he was wrong; and being under-capitalized was a major factor in his not succeeding. He planned to do too much with too little money.

On top of that, he lacked direction. He was not clear on where he was going. The apostle Paul wrote, *"Therefore I run in such a way as not without aim"* (1 Corinthians 9:26, NASB). When running a race, speed may be important, but direction is also key. You can't win two races at once. You must finish one race and then the other. Because Tom lacked direction he was trying to do everything, which resulted in too little of a return.

You And Your Team Need A Plan

Plan for your success! An effective business plan will do wonders in clarifying your purpose.

• Stay on track

First, a plan will keep you, the owner, on track. It will help to focus your time and resources on the key priorities of the business. The plan will state where you expect to be, how you expect to arrive, and when. If you miss your mark, you have the opportunity to get back on track quickly.

• Understand the plan

Second, your family needs to understand the plan. Your spouse and children also need to know where you are going and how you plan to arrive. Any start-up enterprise or operation may require you to spend extra hours on the job. By understanding and agreeing to the plan your family will be more supportive, especially through prayer.

• Share the plan

Third, the highlights of your plan should be shared and explained to your staff. Then they can play a stronger part in helping you achieve your dream. For example, Tom, the real estate salesman, never told his receptionist that former clients were to be given top priority. Instead, an inquiry from a former customer was buried under a dozen messages from cold callers. The blue chip prospect should have been put at the top of the list.

Also keep your accountant, attorney, and other counselors up to speed. This will allow others to give you input about whether your plan has realistic goals.

Effective business plans do not need to be overly complex or contain a lot of flowery language. A good plan is one you and others can easily understand and follow, but specific enough to guide you and your team toward a goal.

How To Begin

Many people are tempted to omit a business plan. In their excitement they prefer to just jump in and begin without doing the proper research and taking the time to determine if their dream is an actual possibility.

As we saw with Tom, this is folly of the highest order and spells disaster from the start. King Solomon understood this when he wrote, *"The wise are cautious and turn away from evil, but the fool throws off restraint and is careless"* (Proverbs 14:16, NRSV).

1. Write out a business plan

First and foremost, before you do anything else, you must write out a business plan.

2. Clarify your plan

After deciding what type of business you will have (sole proprietorship, partnership, or corporation), gain a clear picture of the size business you envision for the future. Do you see yourself remaining small and personal or do you have visions of expanding into larger markets and cities? Will you have a physical or virtual headquarters? What will you offer and with what constraints?

Write out a general word picture of the business that you envision building. This general picture, along with your mission statement, will set the stage for beginning your business plan.

3. Craft your mission statement

Your mission statement should explain in one or two sentences your purpose, what niche you will fill in the market, and what you will do as well or better than your competition.

SECTION 3: Defining Your Business

Your mission statement will guide you throughout the life of your business by keeping you focused and preventing you from going in too many directions at once, which is one of the common causes of failure.

Getting More Specific

Now you are ready to get more specific. Again, you will need to **write things down.** Writing things down forces you to not skip important details and allows you to be more objective by seeing your plan revealed in black and white. The following topics should be outlined:

1. **What your business will do.** (Make a list of the products or services you will offer and how.)

2. **Your target market.** (Identify your expected customers. List needed networking in the community.)

3. **Your expected scope of activities.** (Compile an overview of what day-to-day operations will look like. "See" an average day in your mind.)

Spending quality time on each of these considerations and writing them all down will begin to clarify your vision and help you to decide what parts of your dream are possible and what parts are "wishful thinking." David shared with the people of Israel the vision for building the temple (1 Chronicles 28:2-6); and from that same vision, his son, Solomon, built the temple.

An archer needs to see the target before letting go of the arrow, otherwise nothing will be hit, except perhaps an innocent bystander. If you cannot see clearly what your business should look like, you will not be able to succeed. Many people start by shooting the arrow against a wall, painting a bull's eye around the arrow, and then declaring victory. Unfortunately, their successes are more accidental than planned.

Planning is vital. When Mike and Dona planned to open their plant nursery, they researched what facility would fit into their budget, be convenient for customers, have plenty of space to display merchandise, and have adequate water supply. Additionally, they needed to find and build relationships with suppliers of large trees and ensure that enough specialty plant herbs would be available for customer purchase. All these steps and considerations were absolutely vital to whether they would be able to be competitive and profitable.

Market Strategies

Your plan needs to include strategies that take you from the "dreaming and talking" stage to an actual reality stage. But few people put a strategy in place to back up their words.

There are several areas to study that will be helpful in determining the most effective strategy for your business. Take the time to examine and write down the results of your research under the following areas:

1. Identify the size and potential of the current market.
2. Identify what part of the market you believe you can penetrate.
3. Identify what actions you will take to obtain customers.
4. Summarize how you intend to compete based on:
   • price
   • location
   • service

When reviewing how you plan to provide service, **remember that having the best value in the market is of little consequence unless you have an effective plan to deliver.**

For instance, an expert cleaner of high quality oriental rugs required a person and a vehicle to pick up and deliver the rugs. The owner failed to plan for the time it would take to drive all over town picking up and dropping off rugs, thus requiring most of the cleaning to be done by himself at night. He had failed to plan the true cost of delivery and was forced to work 15-hour days until enough funds were available to hire additional help.

By taking the time to research and write down your plan using the four main points of market strategy, you (and those advising you) will have the ability to determine feasibility.

> **While we do not need to be afraid of competition, we need to understand competition.**

Several individuals wanted to open a Christian bookstore in a small town of 4,000 people. The market was simply too small to support a full service store. Instead of opening what was sure to be a losing operation, they worked out an arrangement with a friend who operated a retail store, taking the back corner in the store for their books, with the storeowner agreeing to ring up purchases. The overhead savings allowed the bookstore to succeed, where plunging into a full-blown store would have spelled demise.

Again, a good example of thoughtful market strategy is exemplified by Mike and Dona's plan for their nursery business. They planned to target mailings to owners of newly constructed homes, touting the larger trees that could be available to give new landscaping a mature look. All advertising featured their competitive advantage, the availability of larger trees and their experienced planting crew. Additionally, they contacted garden clubs and offered to give talks on garden herbs; those talks generated new customers.

Competition

While we do not need to be afraid of competition, we need to understand competition. When facing Goliath, David said, *"Let no man's heart fail on account of him. Your servant will go and fight with this Philistine"* (1 Samuel 17:32). David knew enough about Goliath, the competition, to avoid a direct assault. So, he carefully planned his attack using a sling and stone.

Competition creates both opportunities and threats that need to be addressed. When you understand the best opportunities, you can then focus your energy toward filling the gap left vacant by present businesses.

For example, consider that a city has many independent heating and cooling contractors, but no one dominant firm. In that type of market a new business, using an effective advertising campaign, could thrive.

Opportunities are more fun to contemplate than potential threats, but any business will face pressure from one source or another. Several years ago a Barnes & Noble bookstore announced plans to move into Flagstaff, Arizona, a city of about 55,000 residents. At the time the announcement was made, an old time bookstore and newsstand located downtown felt the city would not accept the newcomer. The local bookstore changed nothing during the 18 months Barnes & Noble spent constructing their store. The small bookstore owner made a grave mistake: he assumed the new franchise would not be accepted because they were "out-of-towners."

However, one year after Barnes & Noble opened, the downtown bookstore was forced to close. The small store failed to understand the threat and take action in advance. The Prophet Nahum predicted the overthrow of Nineveh and warned the city to make preparation by saying, *"Draw for yourself water for the siege! Strengthen your fortifications!"* (Nahum 3:14, NASB).

You, too, must be aware of threats and prepare for action.

Organizational structure

Using an organizational chart to plan for future growth will assist you in knowing when and who to hire to attain your goals.

Bill's business was cleaning high-quality oriental and Native American rugs. He worked many hours himself and employed one worker and a part time bookkeeper, but had plans to grow much larger. Bill wore most of the hats himself: pick-up driver, rug cleaner, receptionist, office manager, purchaser, and cleaning supervisor. He was becoming discouraged trying to cover all the bases.

When he began to complete an organizational chart, even though he filled most of the slots, he began to understand what type of person, with what skills, should become his next hire. The chart gave Bill a hope for a better future.

Here is what Bill's organizational chart might have looked like:

```
                    ┌─────────────────┐
                    │      OWNER       │
                    │       Bill       │
                    └─────────────────┘

  ┌─────────────────┐         ┌─────────────────┐
  │      SALES        │         │   DELIVERIES     │
  │       Bill        │         │       Bill       │
  └─────────────────┘         └─────────────────┘

      ┌──────────────────────────────────┐
      │     RUG  CLEANING  PICK-UP         │
      │   Randall    Rug Cleaning Staff    │
      └──────────────────────────────────┘
```

When leading the people out of Egypt, Moses became exhausted from wearing too many hats. Jethro, the father-in-law of Moses, basically reprimanded Moses by explaining that there was a better way to handle the people's important issues. Without organization and having others share the workload, *"You will surely wear yourself out, both you and these people with you,"* Jethro wisely pointed out (Exodus 18:18, 21-22, NRSV).

Like Moses, we need to plan an organizational structure, not just for the day we open, but to support the enterprise five years into the future.

Your organizational chart can be as simple or complex as you want it to be. It must, however, give you a big picture perspective of your business and where you want your business to be one year to five years down the road. Being organized will help you plan and prepare to meet your goals.

Now, take the time to fill in your own organizational chart:

Financial Plan

A financial plan is also one of the fundamental parts of your business planning. Your financial plan will consist of an income statement, including your projected income and expense, a projected balance sheet, and your estimated cash flow. Businesses regularly fail because owners fail to count the costs and therefore lack needed resources to complete the job.

CONSIDER:

• Before you can begin to accomplish any task, you have to be clear about what you are setting out to do.

• This is true of an artist, a construction engineer, an officer in the army, or a mother involved in home schooling.

• Lack of planning brings delay, discouragement, confusion, sub-par results, and possibly defeat.

SECTION 3: Defining Your Business

• Establishing a good plan for your business will allow you to feel confident and focused on your goals, ensure your team stays supportive, enable your counselors to provide accurate advice, and provide the best environment for your success.

• And remember … the only plan that qualifies is one that you write down!

ACTION STEPS:

1. Write out a plan.

2. Ask your counselors to critique that plan.

3. What steps do I need to accomplish, by when, to be successful?

4. Write out an organizational chart, even if you are the only person working in your business, to help you see where the key tasks fall.

ROADMAP SIGNAL:

STOP: I have no plan or my plan has been shot full of holes by my counselors.

WAIT: I have written out a plan, but my counselors have raised issues that require answers.

GO: I have written out a plan endorsed by my counselors identifying who will do what to succeed.

CHAPTER 9

Defining Your Customer

One of the biggest mistakes businesspeople can make is to believe they can be everything to every person. When we attempt to cast our net that wide, we have failed to define our customer.

We need to ask two key questions: "Based on my product or service, who is or should be my customer?" and "What is the most effective way of reaching them?"

Study The Market

Every successful business has customers. The challenge is to identify your specific target market by careful analysis and study. King Solomon wrote, *"It is not good for a person to be without knowledge, and he who makes haste with his feet errs"* (Proverbs 19:2, NASB).

A CPA, specializing in tax returns, moved into a small town of 2,000 people not currently serviced by a tax accountant. He believed that by becoming the only accountant in town, the entire market would be his; all he had to do was move there and open an office.

Unfortunately, he made the mistake of not carefully reviewing the market. First, he didn't have 2,000 "customers." Given the average of three people in a household, he really had only 650 customers. Next, most of the people who lived in the small town filed their own returns and were not potential customers for a CPA. Of the 650 "customers," only 175 used any tax service and most of those used a low cost service because their tax work was simple. Of the 2,000 "customers," only 35 needed a CPA—too small a market to support the practice.

Advance market review would have told him the town could not support the service; to succeed, his market would need to stretch into neighboring towns miles away. The CPA tax practice was destined to fail before it even started.

Choose Your Image

You need to determine in advance what the best image should be for your business and then faithfully execute that image. The impression created needs to combine you mission, your vision, and what you do best within your target market.

Consistency in offering good products and services that reflect the image you have chosen is critical when developing and sustaining a reputation in the market place. Proverbs 22:1 relates, *"A good name is more desirable than great riches; to be esteemed is better than silver or gold"* (NIV).

A discount store needs to offer low prices, as low prices are consistent with a discount store's image. The store needs to be neat, clean, and very basic so the customers can see they are not paying for frills. In a discount store, you see merchandise piled to the ceiling. Everything is in bulk quantities and you do not even get grocery bags, let alone carry out service. Everything they do presents a low-price image.

An elegant restaurant may charge $30.00 for dinner while McDonald's may feed you for $4.00. Depending on what experience you are seeking for the evening, both may offer a reasonable value for your money. The McDonald's needs to offer decent food, quickly prepared, and served in a clean facility. The elegant restaurant needs to deliver high quality food, well presented, on elegant china, and with impeccable service to win your repeat business. Each must offer services and products consistent with their image.

Borders and Barnes & Noble booksellers both have a large inventory and present their products and service within upscale surroundings. When looking for a book, the staff will walk you to the proper aisle for browsing. Comfortable reading chairs give customers the ability to sit and read a few pages from a prospective purchase. A pleasant coffee and snack shop is part of the store. Everything is designed to provide the customer with a high-end experience. Of course, the prices are higher.

Now contrast those stores with a Bookmen's bookstore: low prices, piles of books everywhere, and a lot of used books.

Both images work. The key is staying consistent with your image.

Narrow Your Target Market

Narrow your vision by researching the number of possible customers that would be in a position to utilize your service or buy your products. By focusing your efforts on a predetermined group of potential customers, you aim directly at the market area that will generate the best return.

> **Focus your efforts on a predetermined group of potential customers.**

Remember, a common trap is trying to be everything to everybody or trying to have everybody as your customer. This strategy spreads your resources and energy too thin and makes you ineffective.

Connor had been a builder for 15 years and wanted to start his own business in a Detroit suburb. He first needed to determine who would be his likely customers. Because he had no experience being on his own, Connor would probably not be chosen to build custom homes. Also, he lacked the necessary financing to tackle big projects, ruling out the home construction market.

SECTION 4: Launching Your Business

He researched the building permits issued and found that over 1,000 room-addition permits were issued in his area during the past year. No single contractor dominated the business. Connor believed that if he could win 1% of those jobs that would create enough work to build a successful business. He began marketing himself as the "add-on specialist" and built a solid business by targeting this market. While he received some renovation and basement finishing jobs, he kept his main target market in sight: the "add a room" market and his business grew.

If he had failed to narrow his market, he would probably have faltered, failing to capture anything.

Test Your Market

Once you have determined your target market, give your idea a test before you forge ahead. Job said, "Does not the ear test words, as the palate tastes food?" (Job 12:11, NRSV). Working through some type of test and asking others to validate your idea is important. The test does not need to be complex.

Wendy and Bill wanted to open a restaurant in a downtown area. They spent time observing the existing businesses. They saw there was some sporadic breakfast business, a brief and intense lunch flurry, and nothing in the evening. They realized the target market was limited in that location, so they opened a restaurant in a more suburban area. Their location was near office buildings that offered evening trade rather than just breakfast and lunch. Simple observation saved them from a costly mistake.

Offer Good Service

Every business owner should have the desire to offer the best possible service. You need to define what you will deliver and then deliver that quality to every customer, every time.

Smart business owners determine not only the level of service they will provide but also the price their targeted market will be willing to accommodate. For instance, Bill, who cleaned the quality oriental area rugs, charged a high price per square foot because his price included a charge for pick up and delivery.

He was losing business on the smaller rugs because the customer was paying a factored-in delivery charge. Bill changed his pricing, dropping the price

> **Find the level of service the market was willing to pay for.**

per square foot, but adding a separate pickup and delivery charge for those who desired this extra. That way, most customers with small rugs could drop them off and save the extra charge while owners of large rugs were happy to pay the transportation service for those 12x12 heavy rugs. **The key was to discover the level of service the market was willing to pay for.**

In Flagstaff, Arizona, a butcher selling exceptional prime and choice cuts was forced out of business due to poor sales. The city just would not support the high-quality meats with premium pricing. The market was satisfied with the regular supermarket meat counters. However, in an affluent suburb of Detroit, a butcher pushes out prime cuts of beef all day. The area demand supports the high-quality market.

Many of us complain about the poor service rendered by many air carriers. However, we have to realize that when the public makes buying decisions, ticket prices and schedules are the only factors considered by 95% of the flying public. Given that, it is no surprise the airlines have reduced service. The market will just not pay for service.

Find The Right Price

Consider Sheila, a business owner who wants to find the right price for her merchandise. She considers her overhead expenses, the cost of merchandise, the service she plans to offer, and her needed income from the business. Determining a price with this method may or may not hit the going market price.

A better approach would be to become market price-based. Here, Sheila would first determine what customers are willing and able to pay, then work to establish a reasonable price. Her expenses would need to fit under that. If her market price is not sufficient to carry her business, then she might not want to open her business at all. She could also choose to adjust the number of staff, location costs, etc. It is all part of planning for success.

How do you find the market price? A review of competitors will give you insight into current market pricing for your type of product or service. If you only match your competitor's prices, you will need to provide an additional incentive for customers to change businesses. For instance, will your future location be better and more convenient for traffic? Will you be able to offer a better delivery service? Otherwise, if there is no real difference between you and your competitor, why will customers make a change?

While lower prices might stimulate traffic and increase business, you will need to develop a large volume to help keep your prices down. Traditional full service real-estate brokers sell property at a set commission and offer marketing, multi-listing, home showings, and assistance with the closing. Other real-estate companies may offer a low fixed fee or much lower commission, but the sellers must do some of the work themselves. These firms have developed a low price strategy, based on lower expenses, and less service delivery. While both businesses can be successful, pricing is targeted toward different customers.

There are two pet grooming businesses in the same city but because they target different clientele, they do not compete. Anna's Grooming is for the budget-minded pet owner. The facilities are clean, the waiting room is small and furnished with used chairs, and the magazines are old. Clearly, not much is spent on frills. However, customers get a good grooming job at a reasonable price.

On the other hand, Canyon Pet Palace caters to the most discriminating pet owner. The receptionist greets each appointment by name and escorts the client to a private sitting room where soft music plays. The dogs receive a special ribbon and scent while the owners receive soft drinks and snacks while they wait. Grooming prices at the Palace are about 50% more than Anna's Grooming, but the extra service and ambience is a draw for upper income customers.

Understanding your personal costs, along with what the market will bear, allows you to resist pressure from unreasonable customers who demand lower pricing. King Solomon wrote, *"It 'is good for nothing' cries the buyer; But when he has gone his way, then he boasts"* (Proverbs 20:14, NKJV).

Advertising That Works

We may believe if we build a better business and offer improved service and superior products that the public will automatically come running. Unfortunately, even if you have the best of everything in town, business will be slow unless you find a way to get the word out. Advertising is simply reaching your potential customers and encouraging them to visit your establishment, buy your products, or utilize your service.

In the book of Amos we read, *"Does a bird fall into a trap on the ground when there is no bait in it? Does a trap spring up from the earth when it captures nothing at all?"* (3:5, NASB).

If you want to set a trap, will any trap do? Traps to catch ants, termites, or cockroaches will each be different depending on which pest you want to trap. Likewise, a trap for a raccoon is very different from a beaver trap.

Similarly, the type of "trap" and "bait" you use will depend on what type of customer you are seeking. While I do not believe you will be setting traps per se for customers, you will need to target

SECTION 4: Launching Your Business

your enterprise carefully to attract the type of customer you desire. And you will need to stay faithful to the vision, mission, and image you have determined to create.

• Determine your goal

Determine your advertising goal prior to starting any advertising process. In an advertisement you can only communicate one idea or phrase that really stays with the potential customer. The key is to determine in advance what you want and need to communicate. Wal-Mart has a huge advertising budget, but the line we remember is "low prices."

• Professional quality

Quality is an imperative for any ad. Whether you are preparing a radio spot, a flyer for neighborhood distribution, or a media ad of any kind, invest in professional writing, design, and production. I have been amazed that a business will spend $5,000 to $10,000 on newspaper ads that are not appealing. For a $500 fee, a professionally designed ad can be produced—making the thousands of dollars invested in follow-up advertising much more effective.

If you are unable to spend on professional design and still do the amount of advertising you desire, I suggest using your money to pay a professional to create your ad while cutting back on the amount of your initial advertising. Better to cut back on advertising than to spend without quality.

Do not let the newspaper or radio station design your ad "for free." You will get a quick job that may look or sound decent when viewed alone, but these people turn out ads all day long. Your ad will end up blending in with other ads instead of standing out. A good independent artist is worth every dollar spent!

• Repeat, repeat, repeat

Advertising running at random times will not work. Effective media advertising must run often to make an impact. Each day the average person sees 85 ads. That is over 2,500 each month! Breaking through the clutter is hard. The desired results will occur only by running the same quality ad, consistently and repeatedly.

If you are on a limited budget, far better to try one ad, well targeted, and support that ad than to try everything at once and run out of advertising dollars. Notice the annoying ads on cable TV — you see the same thing over and over. Why? Because they work!

If you cannot sustain your advertising long term, it is better to save the money and invest in something else for your business.

• Choose your media and method

Every type of media reaches different people. You need to choose your media and your method carefully. Advertising an ice skating rink on the "oldies" radio station is clearly a blunder. Most city newspapers offer regional advertising; you pay for advertisement in only part of the city. Local papers target specific areas.

You do not want to pay for citywide coverage if most of your customers will come from a short distance. A hardware store should consider having ads placed next to the home improvement column in the paper, on the "Ask The Handy Man" radio show, or on cable TV's Home and Garden channel. You may pay more to reach each prospect, but the targeted shot may be worth the cost.

I often suggest that business owners ask new customers how they heard of the business. After about three months, depending on traffic, quantify your responses. You will generally see a pattern that one or two advertising methods work well while others fail to bring results. Only by carefully measuring actual results will you see what works and what does not.

SECTION 4: Launching Your Business

A few additional pointers to keep in mind when setting up your advertisement are:

1. Run your ad only on the days your establishment is open for business. Why advertise in the Sunday paper if you are closed?
2. If you plan to have a lot of text, make sure you have a great "grab the eye" headline.
3. Never run down the competition. Rather, focus on your own positive message.
4. Be clear about how and when you can be reached. I have seen good ads that failed to state operating business hours or a clear location.

CONSIDER:

• When advertising, be clear in communicating to your target customer your product or service (that one main idea), the benefit or uniqueness of the product, and what action you want the customer to take.

• The prophet Isaiah wrote, *"'Present your case,' the LORD says. 'Bring forward your strong arguments'"* (Isaiah 41:21).

ACTION STEPS:

1. Who is and who should be your customer?

2. What advantage do you bring to the marketplace that will attract customers?

3. What image do you need to create in the marketplace?

4. Develop a statement you can make in 30 seconds explaining why someone should do business with you.

ROADMAP SIGNAL:

STOP: I'm not sure who my customers are, and neither do I understand my competitive advantage.

WAIT: I understand my customers but my competitive advantage is not obvious.

GO: I clearly understand my customers and my competitive advantage.

CHAPTER 10

Preparing for Your Financial Needs

I received a call from a business owner, Gabriel. "I need help," he pleaded. "I started my business three weeks ago and I have completely run out of cash."

I asked a few questions and learned that Gabriel and his wife had been doing some retail sales out of their home, making about $20,000 a year part time. They believed the time had arrived when they needed to quit their day jobs and take the plunge to full time.

Leaping ... Off The Edge!

They found a building for their retail store and signed a five-year lease at $4,000 a month, giving a personal guarantee. In addition, they purchased $95,000 of inventory, spent $23,000 improving the store, and another $37,000 on display fixtures and equipment.

The cost of opening the first month was:

Inventory	$95,000
Lease hold improvements	$23,000
Display fixtures	$37,000
Rent (two months due)	$8,000
Utilities, including deposit	$3,300
Advertising	$1,900
Accounting & legal fees	$2,700
Supplies	$900
Insurances	$3,400
TOTAL spent	**$175,200**

They "covered" their starting expenses with the following:

Savings	$24,000
Cash in IRA accounts	$31,000
2nd home mortgage (110% of value)	$64,000
Credit card cash advance	$22,000
Loan from parents	$45,000
TOTAL invested	**$186,000**

On the surface, it would look like they had $10,000 in operating funds to start, but in reality they were already in the hole.

By quitting their jobs, they lost the $5,500 per month they were making, plus they now had incurred a much larger house payment and were responsible for credit card advances at a whopping 19% interest!

In addition, monthly expenses were anticipated at $16,000 per month, including replacing their former salaries and medical insurance. The expected profit margin was estimated to be 40% of sales. If sales were $35,000 per month, the margin would be $14,000, already $2,000 short of breaking even.

The first month sales were $4,000 and $5,000 the second, producing only $3,600 of net income. Unable to pay rent, they never made it into the third month! They lost over $200,000, were forced into bankruptcy, had their home foreclosed, lost both cars back to the leasing company, lost their own retirement savings, and their parents were out $45,000 of retirement savings (adding strain to the family relationship).

The tragedy was that Gabriel and his wife's business was destined to fail long before it opened! Strong planning and solid finances can help ensure that a business gets off the ground. Carefully counting the cost is mandatory before starting any venture. You may be optimistic and want to rush the process, but careful planning will keep you on track.

Before you jump, carefully review the following three key planning financial statements: 1) the cost of opening your doors, 2) your expected income and expense statement, and 3) your expected cash flow statement.

Each of these statements doesn't need to be complex, just complete.

The Cost Of Opening Your Doors

The items below are a helpful list to calculate the cost of opening your doors. Keep in mind that some costs are one-time costs while others are reoccurring costs.
- Building purchase cost
- Improvements
- Equipment
- Showcases and display equipment
- Office equipment
- Office supplies
- Stationary
- Business forrms
- Rent
- Required utility deposit
- Signs
- Vehicles
- Tools
- Telephones
- Fax, copy machine
- Computers
- Insurance (facility, liability, vehicle)
- Professional fees (accountant, attorney)
- Required licenses and permits
- Professional association dues
- Publication subscriptions
- Starting inventory
- Advertising
- Accounts receivable necessary to carry the business
- Cash on hand needed to operate the business
- Other
- Contingencies

SECTION 4: Launching Your Business

Signing a lease, rental agreement, or purchasing a building is the first step. The amount owed monthly is easy to determine. Remember, getting a facility shipshape will cost money. If renting, the landlords may be willing to paint, renovate, and make other improvements at their expense, but those costs will be added to and included in the monthly rental costs.

When considering customizing a space, keep your focus on clearly defining the need in advance. If the facility is for retail customers, approach the space from that perspective. If the space is for production or service work, keep your eye on what is needed to run an efficient operation.

The challenge is to balance the need while ensuring the job gets done effectively. Retail space and restaurants need to be well laid out, well presented, clean, and customer friendly. Going overboard with expensive finishes will shoot the cost up while not providing a return. Your target customer must be kept in mind.

If you are handy and can plan the time, consider doing the upgrades yourself and save the extra dollars to reinvest elsewhere.

Virtually every business requires some starting inventory. A retail establishment or manufacturer may need large inventory, but even service businesses require some inventory. For example, an electrician will need a reasonably well-stocked shop and service truck to avoid constantly running back and forth to the store to pick up items, killing any efficiency.

Your experience should help you gauge the amount of inventory to carry. (In retail, generally three months of projected sales need to be carried.) When purchasing inventory, try to locate vendors that will accept returns for cash or credit. I know one store that opened with $120,000 of inventory. About 65% of the items turned over fairly well, but the remaining 35% didn't sell at all! A year later they were still stuck with around $40,000 of inventory that was eventually sold at a loss. If returns were allowed that stock could have been returned and replaced with items that were selling well.

Consider the ease of obtaining new stock when establishing inventory. One framing gallery was selecting primary suppliers of quality frames and matting material. Two suppliers rose to the top for consideration, but the one that offered a 5% lower price took 3-4 weeks to deliver. Selecting the second vendor that charged 5% more but offered next day delivery enabled the framing gallery to have $20,000 less of inventory in stock, and that cash could be used for advertising or other uses.

Depending on the type of business you open, you may need to extend credit. For most retail establishments, offering credit and debit card options will work fine. Others may need to extend credit by billing, especially if your customers are other businesses. An office cleaning business started with contracts calling for $15,000 in income. Each account was billed at the end of the month with terms of 15 days for payment. Figuring every client would not pay on time, they needed to estimate $30,000 would be needed to carry the accounts receivable, and that amount needed to be added to the start up budget.

Advertising is critical and must be carefully considered in advance. When planning your initial advertising budget, find similar types of businesses and inquire how much they spent on advertising— and what the result was.

You will need to find out what each type of advertising will do and will not do, and how much investment you need to make to achieve results. Opening an ice cream parlor, for example, in a heavily traveled area just across from a large high school may require very little advertising—just good signs and a neat facility.

Depending on the complexity, type of business, and location, the total advertising requirements will change. Many business owners fail to accurately determine the marketing investment needed. They end up throwing money at different marketing campaigns with very little to show for it. Your advertising is as important as inventory, so plan it well!

Contingencies or unplanned expenses will strike us all. A good rule to follow is to plan every opening expense in exact detail, and then add 10% to your starting costs. You must plan for unplanned expenses so they will not catch you by surprise.

Your Expected Income & Expense Statement

Preparing a planned income statement serves several important purposes. First, you have a tool to help determine how much operating cash you require before opening. Most businesses take one to three years of operation before they start providing a return. Over that period of time, you need to plan how much operating cash you will require.

Second, you must develop a plumb line to determine if your sales and expenses are within your plan. If you are doing better then planned, great! However, if you begin to slip, then you can start taking corrective measures before you run out of operating funds.

The list below will give you a way to estimate your profit or loss. You should prepare estimates for each month which can be consolidated into quarterly and annual forecasts. Some expenses will occur every month at a set amount (i.e. rent), while others will be variable (i.e. heating).

- Sales from what sources: _____
- Cost of goods sold: _____
- Employee items: _____
- Staff wages: _____
- Owner's wages: _____
- State employment taxes: _____
- Social security taxes: _____
- Medical insurance: _____
- Other insurance(s):   _____

- Facility expenses: _____
- Rent: _____
- Mortgage payments: _____
- Utility expenses: _____
- Cleaning: _____
- Maintenance: _____
- Trash hauling: _____
- Office expenses, supplies: _____
- Loan payments due: _____
- Repair and maintenance expense: _____
- Accounting fees: _____
- Payroll services: _____
- Banking fees: _____
- Credit and debit card discount expense: _____
- Bank monthly fees: _____
- Sales tax due: _____
- Bad debt expenses: _____
- Delivery expenses: _____
- Equipment lease expenses: _____
- Other: _____
- Contingencies: _____

Most new business owners will overestimate sales at the beginning of a venture. To make a reasonable estimate you need to follow a carefully researched process. Start with your market analysis and what you expect to be able to develop as sales. Next, review what can reasonably be expected to come from your initial advertising. When making these estimates, ask other business owners (even if they are from a different area) how their businesses developed at the beginning. Factor the experience of others into your sales estimate.

SECTION 4: Launching Your Business

Also, determine what additional activities you plan to develop to gain new business, what you will do, by when, and what the expected result will generate in dollars.

Realistic estimates are the foundation of a sales forecast. For example, an effective direct mailing campaign for a heating contractor advertising a $49 tune-up special to 20,000 households may generate a response of 0.5%. That would generate 100 customers, providing $4,900 in initial income, plus additional income from any follow up work.

Most ongoing expenses can be accurately forecasted when they are part of a diligent plan. The key is to review each item and carefully develop your estimate. Actual prices, your personal experience, and the experience of others will help set a plumb line. For example, if you will be using a delivery service to transport merchandise to customers, determine who will do the work and obtain clear definitive quotations, including what geographic area is covered by that quote.

Contingencies need to be about 10% of your budget. Despite the best of plans, something always seems to come up. Careful monitoring of each expense is key, and every time an item costs more than planned, then you need to be ready to reduce expenses elsewhere or accept you will be over budget, which is a dangerous position.

Your Expected Cash Flow Statement

Cash flow is the lifeblood of any business. You need more than a good income statement. That is because a business can have a positive income and still have negative cash flow. I've seen businesses forced into bankruptcy at the same time they were showing profits on their income statement!

Steve paid $100,000 cash for a business (exhausting his cash reserves) that had an active customer base. Customers were billed on credit terms net 30 days. Steve didn't realize that if customers were billed at the end of a month, with payment expected within another 30 days, he needed around $40,000 to cover his cash flow needs.

In planning your cash flow statement, keep in mind the payment terms you are able to negotiate with suppliers. Keep also in mind the words of King Solomon, who said, *"Do not withhold good from those to whom it is due"* (Proverbs 3:27, NASB). Make commitments you can honor and then honor those commitments. Asking suppliers to carry your cash needs, unless terms have been agreed upon in advance, is a violation of your word.

A sample cash flow statement would include:
- Starting cash
- Cash receipts
- Cash outgo
- Employee items
- Staff wages
- Owner's wages
- State employment taxes
- Social security taxes
- Medical insurance
- Insurances
- Facility expenses
- Rent
- Mortgage payments
- Utility expenses
- Cleaning
- Maintenance
- Trash hauling
- Office expenses, supplies
- Loan payments due
- Repair and maintenance expense
- Accounting fees
- Payroll services
- Banking fees
- Credit and debit card discount expense
- Bank monthly fees

SECTION 4: Launching Your Business

- Sales taxes due
- Bad debt expenses
- Delivery expenses
- Equipment lease expenses
- Other
- Contingencies

Total cash received: _____

Cash required by business: _____

Over or under required amount: _____

Where Is Your Cash Coming From?

Determine where the cash will come from after you determine how much cash is needed for your business. Often, business owners start with available cash and then build a plan around that cash. This is OK, as long as the investment is enough to succeed. I have seen too many people start with an inexpensive poor location or fail to invest on advertising due to a lack of cash, and then fail because business did not develop.

Most businesses need some cash to start or grow.

• Raising capital through investors

If you raise capital by getting investors, there are several key factors that need to be considered.

First, investors will want to be informed about every aspect of the business including your plan, your success, and your struggles. Complete honesty is necessary when you ask someone for funds. Moses instructed, *"You shall not bear a false report"* (Exodus 23:1, NASB), and anytime we fail to disclose everything, we have committed the sin of bearing a false report.

A company issuing new stock or bonds is required to fully disclose everything to investors, often in 100-page documents. While your disclosure may be far shorter, you need to be complete. Most investors can deal with risk, but no investor can deal with false reports.

Second, the money investors bring to the table is not a loan. Of course, investors will want some control of the business and a portion of the future profits, but you won't have to repay the investment as you would if it were a loan.

If you are independent and want to remain in control, you need to understand that investors have the right to see and understand your business plan. In fact, the same investors will hold you accountable to execute that plan. The accountability part may rub you the wrong way, but it can actually be very helpful.

Third, investors will expect a return on that investment by sharing in part of the profits. Conflict can arise when there is no clear understanding how profits will be distributed. One investor may want dividends issued while the owner may want funds reinvested into the business. King Solomon wrote, *"Through presumption comes nothing but strife"* (Proverbs 13:10, NASB). Tough questions like profit or loss distribution need to be addressed and agreed to in advance. If you are unwilling to concede some level of control, then do not solicit investors for your business.

• Raising capital by asking friends and family

Asking friends and relatives to invest in your business is better than borrowing money from a bank, but it has its own set of problems. (A good definition of a distant relative is a close relative to whom you owe money.)

If you do accept investments from relatives, make sure that they can afford to take a loss. I have seen many incidences of parents investing their retirement money into their child's business. When the venture fails, the parents are left without their much-needed retirement income. As the borrower, it is your responsibility to not allow an individual to investment into your business what he or she cannot afford to lose.

• Raising capital by getting a loan

Loans are often used in an effort to raise capital, but I do not recommend starting your business with a lot of borrowed money.

If you choose to borrow money, here are several key issues that you should consider:

• Nowhere in the Bible does God ask anyone to borrow money. Instead, He always provided the means when He told someone to do something.
• Debt is not a blessing; it is a curse.
• Debt must be paid back.
• Debt always comes at a price: interest and control.
• Debt can be called by the lender, requiring immediate repayment.
• Business debt often requires you to offer surety.

In Scripture, the Lord always made provision when He commanded someone to do something. When Moses was instructed to build the tabernacle, he asked the people to contribute and ultimately received, *"more then enough for all the work, to perform it"* (Exodus 36:7, NASB). David saved the needed materials and his son Solomon built the Temple in Jerusalem with no debt. And it was a very large project. Another example is Noah, who built the ark without taking out a loan.

Borrowing isn't called a sin in the Bible, but borrowing is certainly depicted as a curse. In Deuteronomy, the obedient are told, *"You shall lend to many nations, but you shall not borrow"* (Deuteronomy 28:12, NASB), but the disobedient are told, *"He shall lend to you, but you shall not lend to him; he shall be the head, and you shall be the tail"* (Deuteronomy 28:44, NASB). Being in business should be a blessing, not a curse.

What's more, debt must be paid back. David wrote, *"The wicked borrows and does not pay back"* (Psalm 37:21, NASB). In a nation where over a million Americans declare bankruptcy every year, this Scripture is very convicting!

I believe there is a difference between corporate borrowing and personal borrowing, but any borrowing falls into the category of wickedness if repayment is not made. For example, if a businessman orders goods on credit that he does not believe he can pay for, then I believe it is deceitful and wrong.

Borrowing will always come with a price. Interest and principle payments are the first part of that price. Additionally, lenders may restrict how you may use borrowed funds or may require you meet certain financial targets lest the loan be canceled. Read the fine print of a banker's loan agreement and you will see who is in control. King Solomon wrote, *"The borrower becomes the lenders slave"* (Proverbs 22:7, NASB) and Paul instructed, *"Do not be subject to the yoke of slavery"* (Galatians 5:1, NASB). We need to be very cautious not to become the slave of a lender.

Also, the lender with little advance notice can demand repayment. Some loans are demand notes, giving the banker the option of calling the loan at any time. Other loans have agreements that require the borrower to fulfill certain obligations. Failure to follow through on these obligations can result in the loan being considered in default and the lender can demand payment.

For example, a friend loaned Stewart $50,000 to start his business. One of the conditions was that if the net worth fell below $100,000, the loan could be called immediately. To verify the net worth stayed above that level, Stewart was required to submit a financial statement to the lender by the 15th of each month for the preceding month.

After a year, the friend wanted his money back for other things, and when Stewart failed to produce statements in a timely manner, the friend called the loan. He had the legal right to call the loan and insist on repayment immediately. It was part of the contract. Stewart was forced to sell the business to make repayment. Habakkuk told the people of Israel, *"Will not you creditors rise up suddenly, and those who collect from you awaken? Indeed, you will become plunder for them"* (Habakkuk 2:6-7, NASB). Creditors have a way of rising up at the worst possible times!

Lastly, lenders often require that we furnish our personal guarantee, or surety, for a business loan. When we give our personal guarantee on a business loan, we are promising every asset we have to repay that loan. The bank or lender can take our home, car, furniture, and savings to satisfy debts. King Solomon wrote, *"It is poor judgment to cosign another's note, to become responsible for his debts"* (Proverbs 17:18, LB). Never, ever, give your personal guarantee on any business obligation without your spouse's informed consent.

As an example, landlords will often require a personal guarantee when renting a building or office space. Equipment leasers may want similar guarantees. Keep in mind that every time you give your personal guarantee, you have pledged everything you own to repay that debt.

Whether you borrow from friends, family, banks, credit card companies, or through home refinancing, a loan is a loan that must be repaid.

• Using personal savings to launch the business

Personal savings are always the best source of money for launching your business, but typically personal savings are limited. Saving money for anything takes discipline, time, and personal sacrifice. King Solomon wrote, *"The fools spend whatever they get"*

(Proverbs 21:20, NLT). Saving to develop a business needs to become a family decision.

With every business venture, it needs to be understood that funds are being placed at risk. There are no guarantees. Clearly understand the business risk and never commit family finances without obtaining the informed and agreeable consent of your spouse. Retirement accounts are also a source of funding but keep in mind that most IRA's have taxes and possible penalties for cashing in. Home equity is often looked at as a resource but borrowing against your home should be seen as a loan. Instead, consider selling the home, renting or moving into a smaller home, and then using that cash from the house to fund a business venture. Selling things accumulated over the years such as antiques, collections, motorcycles, and boats can also produce cash.

Using personal savings to launch your business is the best bet if it is possible. The end result is that you are in control of both the company and the money, which is to your benefit no matter how you look at it.

CONSIDER:

- Do you know the cost of opening your doors?

- How does your expected income statement compare to your expected expense statement?

- Do you know how much cash you really need?

- How are you going to raise that cash?

SECTION 4: Launching Your Business

ACTION STEPS:

1. Complete the form determining costs for starting your business.

2. Complete the forms projecting your ongoing income and expenses.

3. How have you arrived at the income/sales figure used?

4. Who will need to do what to reach that number?

5. Are the expenses calculated from actual experience and price quotations?

6. Determine your reserve funds, the amount available to cover miscalculations.

ROADMAP SIGNAL:

STOP: I cannot create a realistic budget that works.

WAIT: My budget needs work, but looks promising.

GO: I have completed a budget endorsed by my counselors as valid.

CHAPTER 11

Preparing Your Business Location

Seth and Sandra started an art gallery featuring the contemporary work of one artist. The merchandise included bright prints, accessories, and wallpaper borders. They purchased $120,000 of inventory and opened shop. Their start-up costs were paid for and they had a budgeted expense of $10,000 a month with very little money set aside for advertising. The location selected was in an older part of town with most foot traffic coming from a very popular ice cream shop next door.

Six months after opening, their monthly income was between $2,500 and $4,000 a month, far short of the $10,000 break-even point. I met with them to search for solutions.

The location had been selected because of the traffic generated by the ice cream parlor next door and the reasonable rent of $1,200 per month. As it turned out, the location was a huge problem. Most of the patrons for the ice cream store had several children in tow, and while they may have looked into the window, few ventured in and fewer became customers. The art gallery was also located on one of the busiest streets with most of the cars zooming by and with very poor parking. No other business was located close by that would help draw customers.

The galley needed to be located where foot traffic would generate business. Moving was the only option. At first, Seth and Sandra resisted moving, not wanting to walk away from the $1,200 monthly rental payment. I pointed out they were losing $6,500 each month with no end in sight.

A new location was located with slightly less space for $3,000 per month and the move was completed. Total rent expense was $4,200 a month since they had to continue to pay the lease from the previous location. The new place was located next to several other art galleries and restaurants where people tended to browse after lunch or dinner.

Within three months they were breaking even and within a year earned an average of $2,500 monthly profit, completely turning around the $6,500 monthly loss. The difference was the location. Even though absorbing the old rent was a small price to pay for moving on, selecting the right place in the beginning would have saved them over $100,000!

How To Choose Your Location

By examining what happened with Seth and Sandra, you can easily see that selecting the best location for a business is one of the more important decisions any owner will make. It is often the deciding factor between success and failure. *"Can papyrus grow tall where there is no marsh? Can reeds thrive without water?"* (Job 8:11, NIV).

• Determine visibility needs

Start by evaluating potential locations from your customer's perspective. Develop a vision of who your customers will be and determine which location will best suit their needs and promote the best image of your company in their minds.

Retail businesses that require a large amount of walk-in traffic will need a highly visible location. An ice cream store or art gallery may depend on drive-by or impulse traffic to bring in customers, whereas a business selling water purification equipment will more likely attract customers who are already researching those products.

Although a location near to customers would still be important, the water purification company would not be as dependent on street visibility or high-traffic areas, and therefore a high-profile location would not be worth the additional expense.

High visibility or high traffic locations will cost more, but if that is the kind of exposure your business needs, paying for the right location will bring dividends later. Talk to other merchants in the area to

> **Location is often the deciding factor between success and failure.**

determine their level of success. Ask how they are doing and if they would stay in that location given a choice. Monitor the area at different times of the day and take note of traffic patterns, who walks by and when, and how many actually go into the store.

Realtors and leasing agents will often paint a rosy picture, but as King Solomon observed, *"A simple man believes anything, but a prudent man gives thought to his steps"* (Proverbs 14:15, NIV). Ask for backup information to verify all claims. If possible, find out who the previous tenants were and call them to ask about their experience in that location.

• Should you be near your competitors?

Another key issue is to determine whether you want to be located near your competitors. Opening an ice cream store next to a yogurt store, for example, would split the customer base and not benefit either business. However, an art gallery may profit from locating near other art dealers because customers may be attracted to a cluster of similar businesses, thereby increasing foot traffic and sales.

SECTION 4: Launching Your Business

• Consider your image

Determine a location and facility that fits your company's image. A store that specializes in expensive, high-fashion ladies wear will want an upscale location and appearance, whereas a budget paper products store may actually benefit from a "budget" location, reinforcing the idea in customer's minds that they are not paying for frills.

• Traffic flow and parking

Do not forget to check out traffic flow patterns and available parking. Is your location easy to pull into off the access road? Too much congestion or not enough parking will reduce customer visits. Also, verify any road construction plans in the area that would affect traffic. More than one business has set up shop only to have the road torn up for the next two years.

Renting And Leasing

When you have determined the optimum location, look for the most favorable lease or rental agreement. Most landlords will require a long-term commitment secured by a lease. A personal guarantee can also be required when signing a lease. Be careful! A five-year lease at $3,000 per month adds up to $36,000 per year and a whopping $180,000 over the term of the contract, and **a personal guarantee obligates you to pay even if the business fails!** Therefore, you should approach a lease as if you were obtaining a loan.

Remember King Solomon's warning, *"The borrower is servant to the lender"* (Proverbs 22:7b, NIV). You can limit your personal liability by negotiating a shorter term for the lease or by asking that your personal guarantee be limited to the amount of three month's rent.

• Improvements to the space

Most landlords will make some capital improvements to suit a new tenant. Work out the details in advance (before signing any lease) what the landlord will do, by when, and according to what standards. Ask for drawings that confirm the changes to be made and the specific type of materials to be used.

Be sure to budget for any improvements that are your responsibility. If improvements are to be made at your expense, then confirm in writing that the landlord agrees to your plan and whether you may leave the improvements in place when you depart. Some leases require returning the property to the original condition and that can be expensive.

Generally, the more expense taken on by the landlord, the more stringent the rental agreement will be because the landlord will need to recover costs. When possible, you should ask for a renewal option at a set price to lock in your long-term costs. Most landlords will offer an option with some price escalation for inflation.

• Financial considerations

Financial considerations include rent payment dates and penalties along with who pays the taxes, building insurance, needed maintenance, utility and sewage fees, and any association dues. Each of these expenses must be agreed upon and budgeted for in advance.

• Property condition

The condition of the property is important. Consider hiring the services of a home inspector to give you a report before committing to a lease. If you would not buy a home without an inspection, then take the same precaution when you lease commercial space as well. Insist on a thorough property inspection.

SECTION 4: Launching Your Business

You need to consider things such as: Will the air-conditioning and heat be adequate in every season? Is lighting adequate? Is enough power coming into the building to supply your needs? (Increasing power later may be expensive or impossible.)

• Neighborhood safety

The safety and long-term trend of the neighborhood should be taken under consideration. Check with the local police to find the history of crime in the area. Confirm insurance rates with your insurance agent. They can tell you if burglary insurance is expensive or not available at all. Also, carefully review the building for fire risks and determine if there are fire code restrictions.

• Government permits

Government approval may be needed in certain instances. If a health department permit needs to be issued, make your lease contingent upon receiving that approval.

In some locations the fire department must approve any facility storing flammable chemicals. Special zoning permits may be needed. Business signs may be restricted in size, color, shape and lighting, so research any regulations before moving forward. A good sign can increase foot traffic.

Buying

Buying a facility is generally not a good idea unless you already have a well-established business with cash flow. While buying a location instead of making rent payments may seem attractive, most new and young businesses can use their cash more effectively by investing in advertising, increased inventory, or other growth opportunities.

Additionally, making a buying mistake can be far more expensive and difficult to correct than walking away from a lease. In the example with Seth and Sandra's art gallery, they were able to leave an undesirable location for about $30,000. Walking away from a personally owned building would have been much more costly.

Working From Home

With all the advances in computer technology over the past ten years, many people now have established home-based businesses. Working at home typically reduces office overhead expenses, shortens your commute, and offers increased efficiency to the focused individual. Some personalities, however, do not enjoy work at home. You will have to carefully weigh the alternatives to determine whether working at home is right for you.

Wally lived 70 miles outside of Los Angeles and worked in his home, tailoring fine custom-made suits and shirts for clients in the greater LA area. Since business was good, Wally was considering moving from the workspace in his home into a rented facility nearby. In reality, because he traveled to see most clients at their homes or office and had adequate workspace at home, establishing a storefront in his small town would bring in little business, and significantly increase his overhead expenses. He wisely decided to stay at home.

• Check ordinances

Check out your local zoning ordinances to determine whether any restrictions apply. Also read the fine print on your apartment or condominium lease agreement or homeowner's association by-laws for any limitations on doing business at home. Most ordinances and by-laws permit working at home but limit direct sales on the premises, merchandise storage, or having employees in your home. If you are tempted to try and skirt the issue remember, *"Everyone must submit himself to the governing authorities"* (Romans 13:1a, NIV).

SECTION 4: Launching Your Business

Check with your insurance agent to determine whether special liability or property coverage is required. Also, renting a post office box or a personal mailbox can give your business a delivery address and keep salespeople from ringing your doorbell unannounced.

• Image considerations

For many businesses, presenting a professional image is important and therefore an owner needs to determine whether a separate business location is advisable. Accountants and attorneys, for example, may need to present an office-based image in order to be viewed as credible. Other professions, such as Web design, some sales positions, and computer programming, are well suited to work at home. Customers can be contacted by phone, e-mail, or by meeting at the customer's office or a local coffee shop.

• Equipment needs

The amount of equipment needed in the business may also be a factor. In some cases, a person's home cannot accommodate the amount of equipment needed. Perhaps renting storage space would be sufficient.

• Business phones

Establish a separate phone number for your business and always answer the phone in a professional manner. Use voicemail rather than an answering machine to present a better image. Better yet, hire an answering service to take calls when you are unavailable. An answering service can page you or call your cell phone with hot calls. Make sure your fax machine is located away from any bedrooms to avoid being awakened by after-hours fax transmissions.

SECTION 4: Launching Your Business

Do not answer your home phone during business hours to avoid becoming distracted by personal calls. One attorney who works at home was deluged by calls from family and friends because they knew she was there. My advice is to ask family and friends to only call during business hours if there is an actual emergency.

• Work and personal life

The biggest challenge for many people who work at home is separating their work life from their personal life. Establish regular working hours and stick to them. Get up, shower, and dress at a regular time and maintain a schedule. Avoid doing personal business during work hours and vice versa.

Separate your workspace from your living space and establish a mind-set and a habit of working in your workspace and not working in your personal space. Take the apostle Paul's advice and make the most of your time (see Ephesians 5:15-16).

If you need to care for children while working, realize that your efficiency will be sharply reduced and plan accordingly. Work out an arrangement with your spouse to avoid interruptions or limit your work hours to when the children are in school or asleep. Nothing turns off a client or a customer faster then hearing children in the background. If separating work time from personal time is not possible, then that may be a good reason not to work at home.

• Customers in your home

Customer meetings are best held at the customer's location or at a neutral site such as a restaurant or coffee house. If you must meet clients or customers in your home, make sure everything is neatly picked up and you have a suitable spot to conduct business. If family members will be present, inform them to behave appropriately with business clients.

SECTION 4: Launching Your Business

• Planning for the future

Some businesses start out at home because of cost considerations, with plans to move out as income permits. If that is your plan, think through in advance a migration strategy for moving out to avoid staying at home too long. Many businesses have stunted their growth by failing to relocate at the right time. With careful planning and discipline, working at home can be very successful and rewarding.

CONSIDER:

• Where you locate your business and how you go about the details of implementing that decision can greatly affect your bottom line.

• Everything else being equal, the choice of a wrong location can spell disaster while the choice of an excellent location may give you a more generous learning curve with your new endeavor.

ACTION STEPS:

1. Does the location fit your mission and business vision?

2. Create a location checklist and divide it into two parts: items that are absolute requirements and items that are nice to have.

3. Itemize every cost from a perspective of location, rent, utilities, and needed improvements.

4. Document any zoning restrictions that apply and ensure any lease/rental agreement has been reviewed by an attorney.

ROADMAP SIGNAL:

STOP: I cannot find an affordable location that fits.

WAIT: I have one or more possible locations but have not finished my due diligence.

GO: I found a location that fits my customer needs and business vision. It is affordable and my due diligence is completed.

CHAPTER 12

Preparing to Equip Your Facility

Equipping your business facility in advance will help to smooth your path. Begin by carefully identifying what your business actually needs to be successful. (Needs are different from desires, which are those things that would be nice to have, but are not necessary.) The apostle Paul wrote, *"And my God will meet all your needs according to his glorious riches in Christ Jesus"* (Philippians 4:19, NIV). God has promised to provide what we need, not everything we desire.

Your preparation should include: **A**) your general presentation to the customer, **B**) the equipment you need to run your business, and **C**) your required inventory or stock.

In some cases, the customer may see virtually every part of your operation, and special care will be needed to present a positive image in all three areas. In other situations, the customer may see nothing at all, as in the case of a mail order house business.

General Customer Presentation

Before you begin setting up your business, be sure to review your mission statement and vision. You will want to execute your mission and vision in everything that is presented to your customers.

• Exterior and interior appearance

The outside of your premises needs to be inviting, welcoming, and supportive of your business vision. Clean windows, fresh paint, and landscaping send a positive message to your customer. Since the outside is the first thing your customer will see, invest in making everything appealing.

Once inside, focus first and foremost on a neat and clean presentation. Even if your budget is limited, you can keep everything clean and orderly. A cluttered desk sends a message that you are disorganized, which may compromise a customer's confidence.

Keep wall hangings professional and avoid posting jokes, cartoons, or general clutter. Once I saw a posted sign that read, "Call our customer complaint line 1-800-GET-LOST." In another store there was a customer service button mounted inside a mousetrap. Both businesses communicated a very negative message!

Some businesses require travel in order to meet with customers. In those cases, you and your transportation become what the customer will see. Decide what image you want to present to your customers, an image in line with your vision. Your car, dress, and business cards all send a message. It is the small details like placing your papers inside a brief case and wearing the company logo shirt that keep your image consistent and make a good impression.

• Displaying merchandise

When selecting shelves and other methods of display, keep in mind what type of products you are displaying and how it can best be merchandised to elicit favorable customer response.

Make sure all your items can be visualized well. The best way to highlight products is to leave some space around each one. By avoiding overcrowding, each item will stand out. When every square inch is taken up, the customer can become overwhelmed and not see all the items you have for sale. Keep aisles clear to allow people to comfortably browse without feeling cramped.

If you are presenting high quality, specialty products, then your shelving and display case must reflect that vision, as with a fancy boutique. A discount store could use plain display shelving or cases, presenting an image of economy to the customers.

When you are setting up your products, keep in mind the way the customer will need to examine the merchandise. A motor sports store selling four-wheelers, snowmobiles, and dirt bikes will need plenty of space where customers can walk around, touch, feel, sit, and envision riding the bikes. Other types of businesses may best present their merchandise in locked, lighted cases. One reason a jeweler keeps merchandise in a display case, other than for security reasons, is to send a signal to the customer that every item is special and requires proper handling and assistance.

Lighting is another important factor in the proper display of merchandise. Excellent lighting will present the item at its best, while poor lighting will detract from the product's best features. Consider not only the amount of light but the type of lighting as well. Certain lighting may be economical but does it show off your items in the most beneficial way?

It is also a good idea to keep the area near the cash register free of clutter. If you want to add impulse items near the check out area, that is fine, but ensure you have enough space to complete the sales transaction easily. A customer may unconsciously buy less if they feel the check out counter is overcrowded.

Similar merchandise should be displayed together and the products you believe are your best sellers should be given the most prominent location. What your customers see when they first walk in will make a lasting impression, and therefore you should show your best goods immediately. You want to give your customers that "wow feeling" when they first enter.

Placing your best selling items at eye level will also help increase sales as customers tend to notice less often those items closer to the floor or on higher shelving. The floor and higher spaces can be useful, however, for larger items or slower selling products.

As you progress, ask your friends and counselors to give honest, candid feedback as to whether you have successfully fulfilled your vision with your displays. When several people give you the same feedback, the information is probably on target.

• Developing a logo

Developing a logo is an important part of preparing your business. The logo can, and should, be used extensively. Your logo should reflect your company vision and is worth the investment of hiring a professional designer. The several hundred dollars you will spend can produce a logo to be used in advertising, on business cards, stationery, store signs, etc. The best logos are simple, colorful, memorable, and consistent with your vision.

When first starting your business you may not use the logo extensively, but you should still invest in a good logo and incorporate it as you continue to develop your business. Developing the logo early will help save you money in the long run. Placing the logo on business cards now will give you instant impact, and you will not have the double expense of redesigning your cards later. Consistency of image is important in everything you do, as you want your initial impression to be a lasting one.

• Custom printing

Every business will require some printing at start up, such as business cards, letterhead stationery, posters, signs, and customer order forms. Again, you will want to keep your printed material consistent with your business vision.

SECTION 4: Launching Your Business

For instance, an interior designer specializing in expensive custom furnishings would want a high quality business card with raised lettering.

Cards should be easy to read, have your name and address easily identifiable, and have pleasing eye appeal. Avoid the temptation to add so much that it creates a congested look. If you need additional information, use a fold over design that keeps the front simple and readable and then place the details inside. If you are serving a Spanish-speaking customer base, consider printing some cards in Spanish or placing a Spanish version on one side of the card.

Before placing orders, consider—from a customer's perspective—what printed material you will require. If you intend to market using letters, then extra care needs to be taken in the design of your stationery. If most contact will be face to face, then weight your investment more heavily toward printing a more impressive business card.

Keep in mind that customer order forms, sales receipts, and invoices are also a reflection of your business and of you. A sales receipt, for example, is one document the customer will take with them when they leave your store. Even if you buy preprinted forms that work with your computer, consider having them customized, including imprinting them with your logo.

• Signs

All businesses, other than home-based, will need some type of sign. Review your needs and business vision and then order a sign in keeping with those requirements. If customers never or rarely visit your business, then a simple and functional low-budget sign will do.

However, if your business is dependent on walk-in traffic, you should invest in a sign that attracts the eye and encourages customers to visit. It would be an excellent investment to hire a sign design

SECTION 4: Launching Your Business

specialist, a professional who will supply a design in keeping with your vision and created to attract customers.

Customers must be able to easily see your sign from the sidewalk or street and see it in time to make a decision to stop. On busy streets you will need your sign to be extra special so it will stand out from the others. The sign should communicate what you offer and display your logo, a way to start establishing your image before the customer even enters the store.

Another advantage of using professional sign-design companies is they have knowledge of local sign zoning regulations. Most communities and shopping areas regulate the size, shape, location, and character of any sign as well as the amount and type of lighting. You want to be able to take advantage of the best sign presentation while not violating any sign ordinances. More than one business owner has been ordered to change or remove a sign, resulting in unwelcome replacement expense.

Equipment To Run Your Business

Buying equipment that fits your needs will conserve your start-up costs and cash flow. Equipment should include tools that relate directly to customer service and equipment that is used to support your business operations.

Start by making a list of everything you require to serve customers. When you go shopping for equipment and tools, consider your options. Prices will vary and used equipment may be a good choice.

Pete operated a marginally profitable landscape business and decided to buy a deluxe pickup truck at a hefty cost of $45,000, complete with all the bells and whistles. He also bought additional equipment, like a backhoe, that he only needed occasionally.

Pete could have conserved valuable cash by purchasing a used pickup for only $15,000, and by visiting the "Rent It All" company when specialty tools were sporadically needed. Pete's cash withdrawals and hefty loan payment soon pushed his company into the red and he was forced to close his business and go back to work for someone else.

When Bill opened a new restaurant, he financed $400,000 in start-up equipment and needed $6,000 a month just to cover his lease expense. Nine months later, he was bankrupt, largely because of the equipment debt.

At Bill's bankruptcy sale, Sue and Richard bought the business lock, stock, and barrel for only $60,000 cash. By taking over the property lease and making a few modifications, they were able to operate a profitable enterprise, largely because of the much smaller investment required.

It is easy to get "carried away" and not make wise choices when we are beginning a new business. Being human, we can be tempted to indulge our "wants" instead of our needs. The pride of ownership and the desire to show the world how well we are doing can cause us to make unwise choices. King Solomon wrote, *"When pride comes, then comes disgrace; but wisdom is with the humble"* (Proverbs 11:2, NRSV).

• Define your needs in advance

Carefully define your needs **before** you go shopping so that you can resist impulse buying. Evaluate the jobs that need to be done and determine the type of equipment required. Again, do not deplete your reserves by buying new equipment or tools if used or refurbished equipment will do the same job for less.

A new commercial restaurant stove, oven, and fryer together costs $50,000 but could be found on eBay for $4,000. The equipment may need cleaning or could be in a neighboring state, but the savings would more than pay for the all-day trip needed to pick it up. Also on eBay, a nearly new refrigerator/freezer unit sold for half the price of a brand new one. A used stainless steel food preparation table that cost $1,000 new, sold for $175 used. Additionally, silverware, cooking utensils, plates, coffeemakers, and other supplies are often available at lower prices.

I would not advocate buying used equipment only because of low price. Always shop carefully and exercise due diligence, making sure the used equipment is up to the task. You will want to make sure that your gear is adequate for the long haul. Check out equipment thoroughly and obtain any warranties or guarantees in writing. If necessary, hire an expert to help you. If you locate a $50,000 cooking system for $4,000, you can afford some additional expense for expert advice.

The Internet offers a great way to search quickly for lower-cost options and used equipment. Trade publications often list equipment for sale as well as the names of dealers who carry secondhand products. Almost anything can be acquired for a suitable price if you exercise patience and apportion research time.

Used equipment is not just for start-up companies. For many years I was associated with a company that had a standing order to buy all the used file cabinets that our office supply vendor received. Over the years, we saved thousands of dollars while meeting our storage needs. When the Tucson Gospel Rescue Mission needed to expand their facilities, they located used modular housing units that saved them thousands of ministry dollars.

Not everything used or old is a good choice. For instance, I have a roll top desk from 1900 that has been in my family for some time. It is nice to look at but is not a strong, durable choice for my business computer.

• Equipment lease or purchase

In today's business world, you can lease nearly everything your business needs. The key question is, "Are you better off leasing or buying?"

The great advantage to leasing is your cash is conserved at the start, allowing you to keep up with your bills and invest in sales and marketing. However, since interest, debt service, and risk factors will be added to your lease price, leasing often costs more in the long run.

When leasing, keep in mind that every lease is a loan and you are obligated to pay on the equipment you have leased. A vendor will often require a personal guarantee covering future lease payment for new businesses without well-established credit. If the business fails, you are still responsible for the debt personally. Several times I have attempted to help failing businesses return leased equipment to a vendor. The vendors declined either to take the equipment back or to negotiate any payment reductions, instead insisting on full payment.

If you decide to lease, find out if the price for the item is reasonable or if the price has been pumped up. Carefully consider all the terms in the agreement and look beyond the monthly payment. You may be committing to more debt than is healthy.

Also, at the end of the lease, find out who will own the equipment. I have seen many cases in which the vendor still owned the equipment even after years of payments and interest. In that situation, in order to keep the equipment, another lease or outright purchase was necessary. Since used computers have very little value, you have little to lose at the end of the lease. But other equipment, like printing presses, may have an effective life of 30 years.

Installment purchases may be an alternative to leasing in order to conserve cash, but most banks or suppliers will still want 20-30% down in addition to the interest that is added to your monthly installment payments. The main benefit, of course, is you own the equipment outright at the end of the payment schedule. If possible, paying cash and saving in advance for what you need is always the best policy.

Both leases and installment purchases are debt. The prophet Habakkuk warned Judah when he said, "Will not your creditors rise up suddenly, and those who collect from you awaken? Indeed, you will become plunder for them" (Habakkuk 2:7, NASB).

Try missing a few payments and you will experience the pressure of having your vendor knock at your door to pick up your equipment. King David wrote, "The wicked borrow and do not pay back" (Psalm 37:21, NRSV), a serious warning not to walk away from our debts.

Your Required Inventory

Every business will require some type of general office and paper supplies, while other businesses will need to also stock inventory and service parts. When stocking basic office supplies, keep your inventory low. You can always run to the store once or twice a week if necessary rather than tie up your cash by stockpiling supplies. Many office supply stores offer free or low cost delivery.

| What is your inventory turnover rate? |

Once you have been in business for a while and have determined what items you use and how often, then you can stock larger quantities. When the prophet Ezra was preparing the people to return to Jerusalem, supplies were gathered together and *"everything was accounted for by number and weight, and the entire weight was recorded at that time"* (Ezra 8:34, NIV). Inventory control is just as important to us today!

• Inventory turnover time

Understanding the rate of your inventory turnover is important. If you sell 100% of your inventory every two months, then your turn over is six times a year. A simple method of calculating your inventory requirement is:

Frequency of counting + Ordering cycle + Delivery time = Inventory needed on hand

For example, if you count inventory once a month (30 days) and orders are placed each week (7 days) and shipments are delivered in two months (60 days), then you require a minimum of 97 days of material in inventory.

Realistically, though, you will need some cushion. The tighter you can manage your cycle, the less amount of inventory you need to keep. If you check your inventory needs every week, order immediately with a supplier that delivers within a two-week period. Then you will need 30 days worth of supplies, rather than 97.

Most businesses either buy too much or too little inventory. When you do not carry enough merchandise to meet customer demands, you lose sales and have more expensive backorders to fill. Having too much inventory consumes cash that could be used more effectively somewhere else.

Consider the lead-time when reordering and attempt to locate suppliers that can ship replacement merchandise quickly. A quick replacement inventory supplier helps keep your cash investment down. If you need eight weeks to receive goods, you will need to plan a much larger inventory, allowing a longer cycle to reorder.

• Returning unsold inventory

The ability to return unsold merchandise is an important advantage for any business owner, but is especially critical for anyone starting a new business. If you can return merchandise, even if you pay a restocking charge, you can recover all or part of your money.

I had a client who operated a trendy art gallery representing an artist who produced a wide range of colorful products including prints, wallpaper borders, and bathroom and kitchen accessories. All the products were colorful and modern. The art gallery purchased $150,000 worth of merchandise for the initial stocking. As they gained experience they found about 1/3 of the product line sold quickly, another 1/3 sold more slowly, and the remaining 1/3 failed to sell at all, burdening the new store with $50,000 of inventory that was not selling.

The gallery wanted to return the unsold merchandise to the artist and replace it with the products that sold well, but the artist was unwilling to accept any returns. Ultimately, the $50,000 excess inventory was sold at 25 cents on the dollar, creating a major loss. Establishing the ability to return unsold merchandise would have been a wise move!

• Consignments

Some retail stores take in consignments rather than make outright purchases. With consignment sales, the supplier provides you with the items for sale, and you then endeavor to sell the merchandise. After the goods are sold, you pay the supplier. If the goods do not sell, then you can return them to the supplier.

Consignments work well with art, gift, or specialty items. Further more, when new vendors are anxious for you to try out their merchandise, you can offer to carry the product on consignment, giving you the opportunity to present something potentially exciting to your customers without incurring any obligation.

• Inventory control systems

Most businesses today will benefit from a simple computerized inventory control system. Many software package options are available, so check out what is on the market that you would find easy to use. New systems come out every month and many are specifically tailored to a particular business type. Good computerized systems give you information you can analyze to gain optimum business performance.

The most effective inventory control systems are known as point-of-sale software systems and can be integrated directly into an existing accounting system. These systems allow you to input your inventory as received and then deduct that inventory as sold, working directly from your cash register. These systems analyze what items are selling and what items are not, allowing you to adjust inventory purchases and reorder popular products before the shelf is empty.

Before selecting any software systems, shop around and ask advice from others already using the system. Price is a factor as most systems are priced from $1,000 and up. Remain focused on your business vision and needs. For instance, if you are managing a large or expensive inventory, then investing in an excellent system is wise.

Make sure the system you select is user-friendly. The best system available is of little value if you and your staff cannot use it effectively and consistently. Do a test run with the system, much like taking a car for a test drive. Some of the simple systems coordinate with the cash register to keep pricing information and inventory continually current. Other businesses require a system that allows an account to be kept open until a job is finished.

Consider how you receive payment when selecting a system. A cash-only business will not need an accounts receivable feature. Those who sell on credit, however, will want a system that controls inventory while generating invoices automatically and posting information to your accounts receivable system.

For example, an auto repair shop may not know the extent of the work that needs to be done when first starting a job. They will need to open an order and then keep that job open until completed, whether it concludes that day or a few days later. Their system would also need to produce a record of both parts and labor required for the job.

Smaller businesses with limited inventory may be able to use a manual system. Some businesses save cash sales receipts or the tag from merchandise and then post the information manually. Because they carry only a small amount of inventory, they can decide when they need to re-order by "eyeballing" their shelves. If these simple methods meet your needs, great, but an investment of a few thousand dollars in a simple system will pay most businesses a handsome dividend.

CONSIDER:

• Is your facility equipped?

• Is your general customer presentation written down?

• Do you have all the right equipment?

• Do you need inventory?

• Whether your business requires a lot or a little when it comes to equipment and inventory, the key is that you know what, where, and when.

• That way you are always ready, always preparing for success.

ACTION STEPS:

1. Create a list of equipment that is required.

2. Create a list of equipment that is helpful, but not required.

3. Obtain pricing for required items.

4. Check if needed items are available used to fit the need.

5. Determine the amount of inventory needed to serve customers.

6. Is unsold inventory returnable?

ROADMAP SIGNAL:

STOP: I have no list or cannot afford what is needed.

WAIT: I have a list of equipment needs but require further research.

GO: I have clearly defined my equipment needs, determined the cost, and can afford what is needed.

CHAPTER 13

Preparing for Your Employees

Employees, sooner or later, will be a part of almost any business, and aside from your customers, they will be your most important assets. Therefore, it is wise to not hire in haste. King Solomon observed that "like an archer who wounds at random is he who hires a fool or any passer by" (Proverbs 26:10, NIV). If you do not know the kind of person you want to hire, you run the risk of ending up with a "fool" or a "passer by."

Both accurate job planning and prudent interviewing practices are critical components for finding the right people to assist you in growing a successful business. Choosing the best employees for your team is never something you want to rush.

Prudence Is Needed

A great definition of insanity is continually repeating the same steps while expecting different results. In light of that definition, why do so many business managers continually hire new employees only to see the same pitiful turnover results?

"I size people up pretty quickly," Dave, the owner of an auto parts store, once told me. "I don't need to waste a lot of time interviewing people. I'm a great judge of character and I know good help when I see it." Sound familiar?

Dave then went on to lament how hard it was to find good people and that no one he hired seemed to want to stick around for very long. Not surprisingly, the staff at his store did not seem very happy. Yet when I suggested to Dave that he consider some changes in his hiring practices, he replied, "I can't afford to spend all day interviewing prospective employees."

The truth is if he wants to build a winning team, he cannot afford not to take the time.

Preparation Is Required

The organizational chart you created earlier (in Section 3) will be a tremendous help even if you will be the only employee for a period of time. As we have discussed, your chart reflects your future vision for your business rather than being based solely on the reality of the moment. Using your completed organizational chart determine which boxes you will fill yourself and which boxes will be filled by your first hire.

If you will take the time to clarify your workplace needs by writing an effective job description, sorting out résumés efficiently, interviewing successfully, and checking references thoroughly, you will increase your hiring success and build an effective team.

• Start with a written job description

The first step is to establish the necessary qualifications for each position by writing a complete job description. This important step will focus your attention on defining the essential skills for the position and help you identify the right individual for the job.

The more complete the job description, the easier it will be to find an employee that matches. At the same time, a well-written job description should be simple enough to be understood by every applicant. Although you want your job descriptions to be complete, do not get bogged down in too much detail. Cover the basics and make any necessary amendments as time goes by.

The following is an example of items that could be included on a job description for an auto repair shop:

1. Perform service on customers' cars
2. Post cash received on customers' accounts
3. Take, confirm, and clarify customer orders at the order desk
4. Prepare creative advertising layouts
5. Clean every store window each week

A job description for a sales clerk in a retail store might include:

1. Operating the cash register
2. Placing special orders
3. Assisting customers in locating merchandise
4. Interacting comfortably with customers from a variety of backgrounds
5. Deriving enjoyment from helping others

All applicants should receive a copy of the job description so they completely understand the responsibilities and expectations of the job. *"Through presumption comes nothing but strife"* (Proverbs 13:10a NASB). If you will take the time to prepare effective job descriptions, you will save yourself and your prospective employees the grief that accompanies misunderstandings and mistaken assumptions.

It is also helpful to make a note in your planner to review all your job descriptions at least once a year, updating them as needed.

• Define important skills and competencies

While the job description will list the tasks and responsibilities of the job, you also need to determine the skills, competency, and personality traits required for good job performance. God creates each person with valuable skills that can translate into effective job performance as long as that person's gifts match the job skills needed.

SECTION 5: Making Business Decisions

For example:

1. An accounting position would require knowledge of generally accepted accounting principles, accurate transcription of numbers, and a working knowledge of computer software systems.
2. A pet store manager would need good communication skills, a thorough knowledge of animals and accessories, good listening skills, and an understanding of retail merchandising strategies.
3. A firefighter would require physical strength and the ability to respond calmly in emergencies.
4. An automobile salesperson would require strong people and communication skills.

Many managers and business owners rely on an intuitive sense of what is needed in an employee, but taking the deliberate steps of preparing and validating a job description and writing down the necessary skills and competencies will help you become more successful in hiring the right person for the right job.

• Distinguish between requirements and preferences

Requirements are "must have" prerequisites (quantifiable skills, abilities, licensing, or background experience) that make a person worthy of further consideration. For example, a requirement for a dental technician would be professional certification as a dental assistant. For a senior accounting position, you would require certification as a CPA. For an administrative assistant, you might require the ability to process a minimum of 40 words per minute.

Keep your inquiries specific as to skills and demonstrated success in past jobs rather than focusing on the number of years experience. In other words, someone with less experience may in fact be the better employee for your business. More time spent in a particular field does not automatically imply high competence.

Preferences are those qualifications that you would like to find in an applicant but which are not absolutely necessary to do the job. Skills that can be taught to a new employee should be classified as preferences. If you will limit your list of requirements to only those skills that are essential and treat everything else as a preference, you will increase your chances of finding a great prospect for the job.

For instance, if you were looking for a bookstore manager, you would view "previous retail management experience" as a requirement, while "previous management experience in a bookstore" a preference. If you narrowed your requirements to "bookstore management experience" only, you might eliminate someone who has a wealth of other retail management experience and is an avid reader. In other words, you might overlook an attractive candidate.

As long as your requirements and preferences are clear when you begin to receive applications, you should be able to quickly assess the qualifications of each applicant.

• Conduct an effective interview

Before we look at specific ways to develop effective interviewing skills, let us make sure we understand the objectives of interviewing. The interview process is designed to accomplish several things:

1. **Assess an applicant's ability.** Does he or she have the skills andcompetencies to be successful?
2. **Evaluate "manageability."** Will the person accept on-the-job instruction?
3. **Determine level of interest.** Does the applicant want the job?
4. **Evaluate "fit."** Is the person a good fit for your business and management style? Is he or she a team player?
5. **Test for attitude.** Does the candidate have a positive attitude?
6. **Assess communication skills.** Does the applicant possess the necessary communication skills to be successful?

SECTION 5: Making Business Decisions

7. **Validate the résumé.** Is everything true and correct? Are the person's claims of past experience accurate?

• Eliminate by phone first

I almost always recommend that a hiring manager interview candidates by phone first. A telephone interview saves everyone time, obtains basic information, and may eliminate many candidates who do not match your desired profile. The goal of your initial call is twofold: to determine whether an applicant fits your basic needs and to determine whether a face-to-face interview is worth conducting.

Key areas to probe over the phone include verifying items on the person's résumé, explaining the essential requirements of the job, and asking about past experience that may be relevant to the job. Be sure to focus on the actual functions the person performed, not just on job titles, and ask about the most important aspects of the applicant's current job and what has been their most successful past work experience. Make sure to verify that the candidate meets each of the essential job requirements. Otherwise, do not schedule another interview.

By the end of the call, you should have enough information to either schedule a formal interview or to thank the person for their time and explain that their qualifications do not meet your exact needs.

• Conducting the interview

When candidates come in for an interview, be sure to present a professional atmosphere that makes your company attractive to your top prospects. When interviews are scheduled, inform your receptionist or members of your staff so that everyone will know to greet the applicants. Create a warm, personal, yet private atmosphere and do not allow any interruptions. Interruptions cause both you and the prospect to lose focus and send the message that the interview is not very important.

PREPARE AN OUTLINE IN ADVANCE

Prepare an outline in advance with penetrating questions to ensure that you obtain the information needed to make the right choice. Make copies to use with each candidate and take notes to help you remember the high points and low points of each interview. Do not wait until later to write down your impressions of each candidate. Do it as you go along because time has a way of rewriting your memory. Should any of your questions be greeted with silence, always wait for an answer.

ADDRESS THE RÉSUMÉ

Begin by covering the details contained on the résumé. Confirm the starting and ending date of each past job, the starting and ending salaries, the progression within each position, and the raises that were given.

Starting the interview by focusing on the applicant's résumé accomplishes several things:

1. It allows the candidate to become more comfortable by covering familiar territory.
2. It establishes that you intend to be thorough with the interview.
3. It confirms all the important facts on the résumé right up front.

Fifty percent of résumés contain misstatements or false claims. By asking probing questions and follow-up questions, you will improve your chances of finding the truth.

FOCUS ON ABILITY

Discuss their work history in detail to accurately assess their ability. Thoroughly explore successes on past jobs by asking how a feat was accomplished. Be specific in clarifying skills claimed and be prepared to ask candidates to demonstrate stated abilities and skills. If dealing with dificult customers is important, try role playing, taking the role of a troublesome customer to see how the candidate performs. Have candidates demonstrate their ability on machines, computers, or other specialized tasks.

ASK QUESTIONS

Evaluate ability by asking:
- What were the three most important aspects of your job?
- What were your overall achievements?
- What is your greatest strength?
- What is your biggest weakness?

Evaluate attitude and manageability by asking:
- What excited you most about past jobs?
- What was your least favorite part of the job?
- Describe your current boss. What do you like most and least about your boss?
- Tell me about a conflict with a past supervisor and how that conflict was resolved.
- How could your past supervisors have done a better job?
- How does your current boss get the most out of you?
- What have you learned from your last three bosses?
- Explain how your past performance was rated. Was that rating fair?

Your goal is to understand how a person's past experience might translate into future success working for you. If every past boss was a "jerk," if every job the person quit was for "political reasons," and if performance was always rated "unfairly," then you should probably remove the applicant from consideration.

SECTION 5: Making Business Decisions

In addition, part of the purpose of interviewing applicants is to evaluate their communication skills, an especially important qualification for working in a retail environment with customers and staff. To assess written communication skills, you might include an essay question on your application form.

Evaluate communication skills by asking:
- In what way has written and oral communication been important in your past jobs?
- Do you prefer written or oral communication?
- How have you been required to communicate with customers in the past?
- How do you define customer service?

Evaluate the ability to work as a team by asking:
- Have you worked with a similar team? If so, what was your experience?
- When working with new people, how do you get to know them?
- Tell me about a colleague with whom you have gotten along well, and one you have not.
- Have you ever placed another person's work before your own?
- Can you give an example?

At the end of the interview if you are seriously interested in a particular candidate, ask, "Do you want this job? And if offered, how long would you need to make a decision?"

These questions will flush out those applicants who are not really interested and save you the time and trouble it would take to pursue them further.

• Check references

When you are ready to offer someone a position, the final step is to check references. **Do not skip over this step**—the best predictor of future performance is past performance. Always insist on work-related references rather than personal character references.

Character is important, but your objective is to understand how the person performs in the workplace. The purpose of checking references is to:
1. determine whether the applicant's résumé is accurate
2. verify the truthfulness of answers given during the interview
3. gain further insight into how well the candidate will fit in your organization
4. obtain another perspective of the applicant

Scripture states, *"Every matter must be established by the testimony of two or three witnesses"* (2 Corinthians 13:1, NIV). So, make a list of questions and call more than one reference.

WHAT TO ASK THE REFERENCES:

When checking references you will want to verify:
- Any important claims the applicant made
- How the person handled conflict
- If they followed through on assignments
- How they accepted criticism
- Whether they continued to grow in their profession or trade
- What their greatest strengths and weaknesses were

Managers often fail to check references because they think they do not have time, because they trust their own interviewing skills too much, or because they just have trouble asking penetrating questions. Do not make the same mistake. Check references.

CONSIDER:

- Investing the time and energy to find the right person or persons to assist you can make or break your business.

• Hiring and training new employees requires a major expenditure of time and money.

• If you will follow an orderly procedure when filling your staffing needs, you will hire the right person more often than not, and avoid the time-consuming headache of having to dismiss and replace employees who do not work out.

• Think of the process as a treasure hunt—a hunt for the right jewels to glorify God in your business life.

ACTION STEPS:

1. Prepare a job description for each position.

2. List the skills and competencies needed for each.

3. Develop a list of interview questions to use.

ROADMAP SIGNAL:

STOP: I have no job descriptions, but I know what good work is.

WAIT: I know what needs to be done, but have not written out job descriptions.

GO: I have prepared clear job descriptions and determined the skills needed for each position.

SECTION 5: Making Business Decisions

CHAPTER 14

Preparing Your Work Procedures

Two years ago, Tom and Janet opened the Jackson Door and Window Company of Knoxville, Tennessee. Their business represented several high-end window manufacturers and catered to both new homebuilders and the replacement window market. The product line was selling well, reaching sales of two million dollars a year, allowing them to hire two people for up front sales and a crew of two men to perform window installations.

Based on their projected profit margins and overhead expenses, the company expected a profit of $140,000 their first year, a good return for any new business. However, a number of nagging problems were slowly killing the profitability of the company.

First, some of the window measurements taken at the customer's sites were found to be slightly off, requiring either more labor time during installation or reordering of completely new replacement windows.

Second, the sales staff was making mistakes when placing orders, again requiring that products be reordered and the wrong sizes placed in inventory.

Third, windows were being automatically ordered from the manufacturer each time a new window was sold rather than being ordered on an "as needed" basis.

Each of these three areas caused inventory to swell and cash flow to suffer. In fact, the growing inventory of windows now totaled $160,000. To make matters even worse, customers were furious with delays caused by product reordering, which was a three- to four-week process.

Unfortunately, the problems did not end there. The installation crew regularly discovered they had the wrong tools or needed absent tools and installation materials. On the many occasions this occurred they had to return to the shop for the proper tools or stop at a nearby store to purchase what they needed. Each situation cost the company valuable time and money.

A company that should have been generating excellent cash flow and profit was actually losing money and Tom and Janet were being pushed to the edge of bankruptcy. The main reason for the budding disaster was a lack of standard operating procedures, procedures that would have created an easy system for everyone to follow and prevented the problems threatening to destroy the business.

• The solution

Tom and Janet had a clear vision for their business, they had identified a great market niche, and they had done a great job of marketing and selling. But since they lacked an organized operating system, they had nearly ruined their company's chance of success.

A plan to save the Jackson Door and Window Company was quickly set in motion. A step-by-step ordering process was established that each sales person was required to follow to the letter. The procedure began with a checklist that covered every aspect of a door or window, beginning with the choice of glass and including the size, type, material, color, and decorative touches of each product. Nothing was left to chance. When the checklist was completed, the customer signed an agreement that covered the order.

As a result, mistakes were reduced to nearly zero, eliminating the previously expensive errors. Since the salesperson had a checklist to follow, the ordering process was also faster, a nice side benefit of the reorganization process.

Additionally, procedures were established for the installers to follow. Before a crew departed for an installation, they checked the order to ensure each item was complete, reviewed the work site specifications to determine what tools were needed, and checked the supplies on the truck to ensure everything required was available. These steps resulted in more efficient and professional installations as the crew avoided multiple trips from the job site back to the shop or to the store.

The act of developing and rigorously following through with an organized operational system pulled the Jackson Door and Window Company from the jaws of bankruptcy back to a very profitable situation.

Order Is Important To God

An orderly process is important to the Lord and **therefore an orderly process needs to be important to you** as you set up your business. You will want to establish operating procedures, for every aspect of your business. By writing out your procedures both you and your colleagues will be able to follow the procedures every time with consistency.

The Lord demonstrated the need for order in His people when He spoke through the prophet Amos saying, *"Thus He showed me, and behold, the Lord was standing by a vertical wall, with a plumb line in His hand"* (Amos 7:7, NASB). A plumb line was a simple tool consisting of a string with a weight attached that could be hung straight down. A builder could build a straight wall by following the line.

McDonald's has procedures covering every aspect of making food. Their operational system establishes how food is stored, how long it is cooked, how sandwiches are assembled and even the amount of catsup and mustard to be added. Every detail is covered. Customers have a clear expectation of what they will receive at a McDonald's and the staff is efficient in executing the work. The result is a profitable business, both for the franchise owners and for McDonald's at large.

Write Down Your Business Procedures

Look at each position in your business, each key job that will need to be done, and then write a short procedure. The process of writing out procedures for your business not only clarifies the best way to execute your business vision, but also allows you to train new employees faster and more effectively. Since you have determined in advance the most efficient way to serve your customers, the staff will be able to provide high quality service every time.

Each business will be different. The key point is to determine, write down, and then communicate your procedures for each job.

King Solomon wrote, *"Whether a tree falls toward the south or toward the north, wherever the tree falls, there it lies"* (Ecclesiastes 11:3b). When a lumberjack cuts down a tree, he must plan ahead to cut the tree in a way that makes removal easy. Developing and implementing work procedures is your way of "ensuring each tree falls where you need the tree to fall," not just wherever it happens to land.

Jackson Door and Window established a standard procedure for placing orders. The entire order form was to be completed in full. Failure to complete the entire form, to take a short cut, was a violation of the job standard. An employee would be subject to discipline or termination if the process was not followed.

Unless completing the form in total is a written job standard, clearly communicated to each staff member, then taking any disciplinary action if the procedure was not followed would be unfair. **Holding people accountable for a measurement that has not been communicated will not work.**

For example, a retail store may want to establish a simple procedure at the checkout counter. In addition to ringing up the sale, staff may be instructed to ask several questions such as, "Did you find everything you were looking for?" "How would you like to pay for the merchandise?" and "Would you like your receipt in the bag?" Depending on the type of merchandise, instructions on how to pack an order may need to be included in your written procedure.

Another example is determining how you would like your telephone answered and instructing the staff accordingly. At Jackson Door and Window Company, the staff is asked to answer the phone with, "Good morning, Jackson Door and Window. How may I help you?" This sounds more inviting and less dry to the customer than merely saying, "Jackson Door and Window."

• Be specific

You will need to be very specific in your job descriptions. Again, this helps your employees stay on target to fulfill your vision and also provides you with a tool of accountability.

Keep in mind that something that may be obvious to you may not be apparent to others. Study the procedure sample below that is an example of a written job procedure for a motel cleaning person following the check out of a patron:

1. Knock on door; wait for a response to ensure patron has checked out
2. Open drapes and turn on lights
3. Check for any left items and take them to the manager

SECTION 5: Making Business Decisions

4. Inspect room for any damage; report any damage immediately to manager

5. Remove towels and sheets and place in laundry basket

6. Dust all surface areas

7. Remake bed with fresh sheets

8. Replace all lamps, clocks, television remote and other items in proper place

9. Clean all tile bathroom surfaces with cleaner; wash out toilet bowl, bathtub and sink; ensure all stains are removed

10. Replace shampoo and conditioner if used

11. Replace towels in towel holders

12. Check if light bulbs are burned out

13. Vacuum all carpeted areas

• Establish quality through written procedures

Quality products and services will bring customers back for more, while spotty quality will cost you customers. Hops, a mid level restaurant I visit, has excellent procedures in place to make certain each guest has a good experience. One of the Hops standards is that each guest will be greeted within three minutes of being seated and asked what they would like to drink. If the server assigned to that table is unavailable, the hostesses or manager is expected to step in. By establishing a three-minute standard, each team member knows customers are to be greeted quickly.

In addition, a set standard determines such things as the temperature of the grill and how long each cut of meat should be cooked, depending on how well done the customer has requested their meat. As a result, the food is very consistently prepared.

Another standard has been established to serve the customer his or her meal within two minutes of it being placed on the "out counter." If the assigned server is not available, another team member or the manager delivers the order. Everybody is responsible to pitch in and deliver meals quickly. All staff is held accountable to help meet this standard.

I know of another restaurant that charges premium prices but provides inconsistent service. The quality of the ingredients is high, but there is no set definition for a medium rare steak, so customers receive a variation on different visits. Also, since only the server delivers meals to the table, with no one else assigned to pitch in if the server is busy, your plate may sit on the "out counter" between five and seven minutes. A lack of clear standards leads to a lack of clear consistent delivery, and ultimately, loss of business.

CONSIDER:

• Having specific written business procedures will keep you focused, allow things to be implemented in an orderly and effective manner, help your employees know what you expect of them, and give measurable standards of accountability.

• After you have documented your procedures, review them periodically to determine if your needs have changed or if you have any better ideas. Include your staff in these brainstorming sessions.

ACTION STEPS:

1. Prepare a flow chart of your work processes identifying each step and what must occur by when at each step.

2. Write out procedures for each key task, including standards that must be hit.

3. Validate that the procedures, if accomplished, will fulfill your business vision.

SECTION 5: Making Business Decisions

ROADMAP SIGNAL:

STOP: I know the work, and don't need to write any procedures out.

WAIT: I have identified the key tasks, developed an understanding what needs to be done, but have not put that information on paper.

GO: I have written out clear defined procedures including standards for key tasks.

CHAPTER 15

Working God's Plan

Planning is the important first step, but it is only the first step. It is not the end game.

Clay and Don became partners and opened a small party supply store in Dallas, Texas. The first few months went according to plan, but then problems developed. Some of the employees lacked the "oomph" and struggled to help customers. Money was spent on advertising to bring in customers, but Clay and Don were not sure what advertising was working and what wasn't. Clay wanted to increase advertising above the budget, while Don wasn't so sure.

Party balloons were a popular item, but often staff either overfilled or under-filled the balloons causing customer complaints. Some merchandise sold well, while other items sat on the shelves. The reality was that some things were working well and others were not. Adjustments needed to be made as Don and Clay gained experience.

Establishing a system to work your plan will help elevate you to long-term success. A sailor navigating over hundreds of miles will need to make regular course corrections. The sooner the skipper knows they have drifted off course, the sooner the correction can be made and the less time is lost by drifting off target. Keep in mind that mid-course corrections are to be expected and the sooner made the better.

Coaching And Evaluating Staff

When you team starts working you will need to invest time and effort to ensure their work is on target. Even those hired diligently with good job descriptions will drift off course. Effective on-the-job coaching and evaluations are an imperative element in running a business.

In the training process people learn best when they see you perform the work. Then you watch them perform the tasks, following up with written instructions. Clarity of instruction will help avoid future problems. In the Bible there was a season when *"every man did what was right in his own eyes"* (Judges 17:6, NASB). The results were disastrous. On the job, everyone cannot do what is right in their eyes, **but what is right in the boss's eyes.**

To coach and train, you must *"deal gently with the ignorant and misguided"* (Hebrews 5:2, NASB). Most people want to do a good job and please the boss. Your kind, gentle coaching will help them learn. It is best to point out the need for improvement promptly. Do this, if at all possible, privately, and **never, ever, correct an employee in front of a customer.**

We are told to *"encourage one another"* (Hebrews 3:13, NASB); your positive encouragement for a job well done is as important as correction. Threatening, which includes yelling, screaming and other forms of intimidation, will always fail at encouraging your employee's success at work. If you have a serious problem with certain employees, sit them down, explain the issue, explain what behavior must change and by when, and the consequences that will apply if they fail to change. Serious or repetitive problems need to be addressed in writing, but you should consider making a note for your personal file of any material discussions you have.

Coaching includes regular evaluations. These should be done within the fist 30 to 90 days a person is on the job, and then semi-annually or annually. Evaluation forms can be purchased from local office supply stores.

When completing evaluations, focus on the quality and quantity of work as well as dependability. Use specific examples as much as possible and highlight the best work accomplished.

King Solomon was a great model and wrote, *"Not only was the Teacher wise, but also he imparted knowledge to the people"* (Ecclesiastes 12:9a, NIV). As you have the heart of a teacher, you will

> **Most people will receive constructive criticism better when balanced with positive feedback.**

be able to encourage your staff to grow into an effective team.

Sticking To Your Budget

When you established your financial plan, predictions were made for expenses, income, and cash flow. The responsibility of all business owners is to monitor these factors constantly. Any drop in expected income or increase in expenses will impact your operation very quickly.

Don't wait until the end of the month's accounting report to determine if your sales are on track. Review daily and weekly reports to determine how sales develop. Especially in the beginning, you may need to take quick action if sales are slow.

Spending more than your budget allows can be fatal. Always gauge how your spending will impact your bottom line. If you believe you need to spend on an unbudgeted item, find a budgeted item that you can reduce or delete. Watch any spending items that seem to run high, like electricity. If you have underestimated the electric bill, you may need to reduce your expenses elsewhere.

Also, watch your cash flow. A prospective customer may offer to buy $25,000 of merchandise, but require 60 days credit. You need to determine if you have the cash to support the time needed to collect your money.

Finding Your Critical Success Factors

Every business needs to understand the key success factors that will determine the victory or defeat of a business. Determine the top five factors that will decide if you will be successful, then quantify and measure those factors.

Package delivery services understand that the percentage of shipments delivered in good condition by the promised delivery time is a critical success factor. Slipping even a little bit can aid your competition and cause your market share to be lost.

Mark owns Bayou Plumbing and Heating and has determined several critical success factors for his business. The factors developed include:

- The number of new customers calling to schedule work
- The number of repeat customers that call for work
- The percentage of time a work crew is able bill for customer services
- The amount of service calls that need to be repeated to correct previous work
- The percentage of service calls made within the promised time
- The percentages of larger bid jobs won

He maintains a log of customers serviced, noting which are new and which are old customers. Mark needs about 100 service calls to keep his crews busy. One way to get those calls is to advertise and then track the results. In his log he makes a note about how customers heard about Bayou Plumbing and Heating. If the number of service calls starts to drop off, Mark knows where to spend his advertising dollars for immediate results.

In addition, Mark needs each crew to be able to bill a minimum of 50% of the time they are on the job. That includes travel time, getting supplies, unexpected delays, etc. Each crew is rated as to the percentage of time that is billable and that information is logged as well.

Mark doesn't need to wait for the accounting report to determine if the month is profitable because he already knows the percentage of time billed, the number of service calls that month, and how his advertising is working.

When dealing with follow-up calls, which are an expense, Mark encourages each crew to do the work right on the first call and expects a thoroughly completed job. One follow-up call in 25 is the number that Mark tries to beat. If it is more frequent than that, expenses increase.

When work is scheduled, Mark takes it very seriously. He knows that over-scheduling results in increased expenses and dissatisfied customers. He works with the individual who schedules the appointments so that 96% of all service calls are handled within the promised time. If a crew is late, Mark absorbs the overtime costs rather than miss the agreed service day. He logs this information as well.

Mark bids on five to 10 larger jobs each month, work that takes from two days to two weeks to complete. Since his goal is to win 25% of the bids, if he starts losing more, he reevaluates the method of preparing bids.

The key for Mark's business is to determine what success factors apply to his business and then make certain that he does precisely what is required to succeed. Measuring his results is a major part of guaranteeing that success.

Learn From Failures

One of the most painful realities of business is that not everything will work. Despite the best planning and execution, we will experience failure in something we do. The key is to learn from everything that goes wrong and not repeat the same lesson again. King Solomon wrote, *"For a righteous man falls seven times, and raises again"* (Proverbs 24:16a, NASB). We will all stumble and fall, but we must move forward and learn from mistakes and failures.

When something doesn't work well, develop the habit of pinpointing what went wrong, and why. Ask yourself what changes need to happen to correct the problem.

Jessica operated an interior home decorating business. Business was slow and customers too few. She tried several methods of advertising with minimal results. She kept trying new ways of connecting with customers, including mailing to new homeowners in her area. That program worked and quickly propelled her business.

Jessica had planned to budget a significant amount of money for advertising, but she had to try several different approaches before success came.

Some efforts need to be abandoned, as King Solomon understood when he wrote, *"A time to search, and a time to give up as lost; a time to keep, and a time to throw away"* (Ecclesiastes 3:6, NASB). Generally, when an effort is not working and we cannot figure out a solution, we may need to abandon the activity.

I know of an ice cream stand that was doing good business, but the main highway through town was moved, and as a result, the steady flow of customers stopped. The owner could have kept going until the cash ran out, but he understood that he needed to either move to the new highway or close up. He chose to move.

When you experience difficult decisions like these, recognize that cutting your losses is part of the game. When the fish farm I invested in was sinking like a rock, I was given the opportunity to receive 30 cents on the dollar for my investment. I took the offer and salvaged something. I lost a lot, **but I didn't lose everything.**

When money is spent, and the results are disappointing, recognize that the money spent is gone. A common mistake is to keep putting more money into a bad situation. That is not wise! Salvaging something may be the best option. The prophet Amos wrote,

"A shepherd saves from the lion's mouth only two leg bones or a piece of an ear" (Amos 3:12, NIV). If a wolf grabs your lamb and you can only recover two leg bones, then accept that, given the circumstances, that's not a bad result.

King Solomon observed, *"If you falter in times of trouble, how small is your strength"* (Proverbs 24:10, NIV). Challenges will come and discouragement will threaten to overwhelm you. At those times, you need to be clear about whether you were called into your business by the Lord, or by your own ambition. That clarity will help you get through, as Paul wrote, *"We are afflicted in every way, but not crushed; perplexed, but not driven to despair; persecuted, but not forsaken; struck down, but not destroyed"* (2 Corinthians 4:8-9, NRSV).

CONSIDER:

• Do you feel you have what it takes to "coach" employees?

• How is your budget? Is it clearly defined?

• List your critical success factors here:

    1: _____

    2: _____

    3: _____

    4: _____

    5: _____

ACTION STEPS:

1. List your critical success factors here:

    • _____

    • _____

SECTION 5: Making Business Decisions

- _____
- _____
- _____

2. Identify three mistakes you have made, and what you learned from each.

3. Match you income to budget each week for 60 days and determine why you are above or below budget.

ROADMAP SIGNAL:

STOP: I have no budget, or the ability to monitor a budget, and haven't a clue to my critical success factors.

WAIT: I have a budget but am unclear how to monitoring or am not clear what the key success factors are.

GO: I have identified and am able to measure at least three critical success factors and my budget is in place ready for monitoring.

Conclusion

There is no conclusion to your business or to the incredible things that God has planned for you. You can rest in that.

I do suggest that you re-read the chapters you feel you need to master so that you are better equipped for success. Business partners and key employees should also be on the same page with you, with your business decisions, and with what you learn from this book.

I wish you the best as you pursue your dreams!

Do you have a right relationship with God?

Without a right relationship with God our lives are very distant from Him, so distant that we do not even know who He is. This great distance causes us to go our own way, which causes further distance from what He intended for our lives. This spiritual separation causes us to constantly feel unsettled physically, emotionally, and intellectually. You may never have realized this connection before. Enjoying a rich relationship with God is the foundation for every other area of our lives, including our family, friends, and business.

An understanding and acceptance that God loves us and wants to be close to us is the beginning of all wisdom and true contentment (John 3:16). Jesus died for our willful disobedience going through life our own way. You know you have fallen short, right?

His free gift of peace, purpose and abundant life eludes us until we recognize that we are each separated from Him and His ways through our disobedience, which is called sin. Yet Jesus paid the price for our sinful nature while we were in a sinful attitude of mind and deed (Proverbs 14:12, Romans 6:23).

God provided a way for us to close the gap between Himself and mankind with the death of Jesus on the cross. Jesus paid the penalty for our sinfulness and showed us how to live a life in right relationship to Him (I Peter 3:18).

The choice is ours. Each of us knows if we have a right relationship with God or not. But we may not all know how to have this for our own lives. God has given us a free choice – follow Him for an abundant life of forgiveness, peace, purpose and fulfillment eternally, or to continue on our own way which brings destruction to ourselves and others. If we are genuinely sorry for disobeying God, are willing to turn from our own ways to follow Him, and then daily, moment-by-moment, allow Him to direct our lives as Lord and Savior, we will have a right relationship with Him for all eternity (Romans 10:9, Revelation 3:20).

These are the steps to a right relationship with God:

1. Admit your need of God and tell Him you are sorry for your sinfulness.

2. Be willing to turn from your sinfulness and turn toward Him (I John 1:9).

3. Believe by faith that Jesus, God's Son, died on the cross, rose from the grave, and now offers you forgiveness of sin (Ephesians 2:8-9).

4. Invite Jesus Christ to come into your life and to take control of your life through the Holy Spirit (Revelation 3:20).

Someone is waiting right now to answer your questions, pray with you, and help you to know how to lead a life pleasing in right relationship to God through Jesus Christ. You do not need to wonder, or continue thinking that if you are a good person God will forgive you and offer eternal life. You can know for certain. If you have never understood this before, or have unanswered questions, I pray you will call **1-888-NeedHim**. Only God knows the span of our life, tomorrow may be too late. Do not put it off another minute. Enjoy a new life with Christ!

NOTES:

NOTES:

NOTES:

NOTES:

NOTES:

CROWN FINANCIAL MINISTRIES
True Financial Freedom

Crown Financial Ministries, founded by Larry Burkett (1939-2003) and Howard Dayton, offers a comprehensive financial teaching ministry. The church program includes the small group studies for people of all ages, seminars, leader training workshops, and budget coach training. The available books, resources, and electronic tools address the financial needs of people in all stages of life. Materials for single parents and those needing career guidance are also available. And through business seminars and a partnership with Fellowship of Companies for Christ, Crown has expanded its outreach to the business community.

BUDGET COACHES

Need additional help on budgeting and debt issues? Thousands of lay budget coaches volunteer their time to assist individuals in developing a budget and reducing debt. You also can become a Crown volunteer budget coach in your church or community.

NEWSLETTER

The award-winning *Money Matters* newsletter offers timely articles and advice on a range of economic and financial topics every month. To help save printing and postage costs, an electronic version of the newsletter, *Money Matters Online*, is also available.

INTERNET

Crown's Web site, **Crown.org**, is the convenient online source for a wide array of financial articles, online tools, radio programs, and free materials for individuals and churches.

CHURCH PROGRAM

One of the primary goals of Crown is to suport the local church with materials and services that allow them to reach and teach their people with God's financial principles. Crown's church program is a collection of dynamic studies that will transform the mind and heart of the local church. Specialized resources for ministering to single parents are also available.

RADIO

Radio is one of the most exciting ministries from Crown. Informative and always entertaining, you can listen to these programs online or via 1,500 radio outlets around the world.

INTERNATIONAL

Used jointly with evangelism, Crown's International Division is training leaders in the far corners of the world to teach God's financial principles to their friends and neighbors.

For details on these and other ministry products and services, visit us online at Crown.org.